BETTER GOLF

BETTER GOLF

The Mental Approach to Winning

by

Johnny M. Anderson

W H ALLEN
PLANET

BETTER GOLF - The Mental Approach to Winning

Idea, design, and production by
Johnston Co-editions
Gothenburg, Sweden.

World copyright (c) 1989 Johnston Co-editions

First published in Great Britain in 1989 by
Planet Books, a division of WH Allen & Co Plc,
44 Hill Street, London WIX 8LB

ISBN: 1-85227-046-2

Design and photography: Nils Hermanson
Artwork: Lennart Molin
Cover photography: Turlough Johnston

Reproduction by Repro-Man, Gothenburg, Sweden

Typesetting by CONCEPT Communications,
Crayford, England

Printed and bound in Italy, 1989, by
Grafedit S.p.a., Azzano S.P., Bergamo,
by arrangement with Graphicom, Vicenza

British Library Cataloguing in Publication Data
Anderson, John.
Better Golf: the mental approach to winning
1. Golf. Psychological aspects.
I. Title
796.352'01

CONTENTS

PREFACE   *Page*   6

Chapter 1   THE MENTAL APPROACH   *Page*   9

Chapter 2   PRACTISING   *Page* 33

Chapter 3   PUTTING   *Page* 45

Chapter 4   THINK RIGHT, CHIP WELL   *Page* 67

Chapter 5   HOW TO APPROACH APPROACH SHOTS   *Page* 79

Chapter 6   ON THE FAIRWAY   *Page* 91

Chapter 7   PLAYING FROM SAND   *Page* 119

Chapter 8   IT'S NOT TOUGH IN THE ROUGH   *Page* 137

Chapter 9   PLAYING, COMPETING, WINNING   *Page* 153

PREFACE

Nobody – not even the present leader of the Golf Tour – is the perfect golfer. In fact, the words ''perfect golfer'' are a contradiction in terms, because the whole idea of golf is that you play the game in conditions that vary from round to round. One day, your swing is working well and you are in a fine and confident golfing mood; your score reflects these happy circumstances. The next time you are out on the course, nothing goes right: your swing is all over the place and your confidence is at zero. Even so, you have to keep your head, not give up, but work to achieve the best possible score, given your level on that day.

Let's admit it: this is one of the things that makes golf the fascinating game that it is. You can never be consistently good or consistently bad at this game. That is why even the top golfers practise regularly, with planned and intensive training sessions, and regular consultations with a teaching professional. All golfers, from the top players to the weekend high-handicappers who want to be able to keep their end up in a game, must practise to maintain or improve their proficiency. And many players do. And still, on that decisive hole, when the chips are down (if you'll pardon the ancient pun) and the game is within their grasp, it is remarkable how many players choke – their game simply collapses – and a player whose technique is not necessarily better wins, simply because he can keep his game together. Why is this?

The answer is ''the fourth fundamental''. Excellence in any sport depends on four fundamentals: knowledge, understanding, technical skill, and mental attitude. The first three are self-evident and fairly straightforward. The fourth is not so easy to learn, because it has to do with the psychological aspects of playing well, and this is still an area about which we know too little. What we do know, however, is that, all other things being equal, the player who has trained his mind has a better chance of winning than the player who has not.

This book is built on my experience as a golf professional over many years. Once a golfer has learned the basic strokes and established a reasonably sound technical game, he must improve his mental attitude. He comes to me and complains that he is losing against players that he knows do not swing as well. I have found that mental training is the answer: I must teach him to be able to program his mind to see the successful result of his shot *before* he plays it. I must teach him to think in the present tense when he plays: not to be downcast by a bad shot, over-elated by the last birdie, or worried about the second-next hole. I must teach him to increase his concentration, so that he can close out everything except the stroke to play. These are the things that will be decisive when he meets players of his own class, and to teach him these, I have brought together the best ideas that have developed in recent years. Teaching ''mental golf'' is not easy, because I must first persuade the golfer that it will work: there is an in-built mistrust towards anything that is called ''mental''. But once they have tried it for a few weeks, golfers find that it improves their attitude to the game, deepens their understanding, and helps them to play better golf. And better golf is what I would wish for everybody who loves this wonderful game, and this is why this book was written.

I dedicate this book to all those whom I have taught and who have taught me.

Johnny M. Anderson

FOREWORD

Some years ago, in pursuit of a winter golf column for my paper, I attended a course on the mental side of sport held in a large house in Hampstead.

That wet weekend, my eyes were opened to a subject I knew little or nothing about. I learned about quiet places to which I could take myself, through my mind's eye, when I was angry or hurt, disappointed or worried. I discovered the left brain and the right brain. I was taught ways of uncluttering both my mind and my body. I did exercises to overcome any feelings of embarrassment I felt at playing golf in front of spectators. One exercise, I remember, required standing on one leg while thrusting both arms out sideways. All the while, music wailed in the background.

I was intrigued. It made me think and talk about the mind, which is something that many people deem to be as inappropriate a subject for discussion as politics, religion, or money.

It is encouraging to read a golf book that covers not only the inches from the tee to the green but also those between the ears, which are often said to be the most important of all in a game of yards, feet, and inches.

I commend this book. All golfers who are prepared to devote time to following its principles should come to believe more in themselves and improve their game.

John Hopkins, golf correspondent,
The Sunday Times

CHAPTER 1

THE MENTAL APPROACH

Why do so many golfers seem to want to avoid any discussion of the mental side of their game? It is very simple to get them talking about the physical side of their game, how they practise their swing, their tendency to slice or hook, what advice their golf pro has given them about practice, and so on. Indeed, it is often difficult to get them off the subject! But if you ask how they practise the mental side of their game, they give you a blank stare or shrug their shoulders. Perhaps they are a little frightened of anything that has to do with the word "mental"! But mental attitudes are very important in golf, and indeed not only in golf, but also in everyday life. A good technical game will fall apart under pressure if it is not complemented by the right mental attitudes. Once you have established a reasonably sound basic game, with a reliable swing, and you want to improve your scoring ability, you must develop the mental side of your game.

Why does a golfer with a sound technique fail to win against a player who is not as skilful? The usual answer is that the winning golfer has greater awareness of each particular situation that he or she runs into on the golf course, has the ability to overcome nervousness, and can relax from the game when necessary. The winner can switch on and switch off concentration at will. This increases his confidence in his own ability, which helps him to play better shots and, therefore, enjoy the game more. The relaxed and confident player plays within his ability level, and, therefore, makes less mistakes and plays fewer stupid shots. That is why he wins more often. These qualities are not the birthright of just the scratch players. *All* golfers can improve their game by training their minds.

If those sand bunkers were not there, you would approach this shot in a much calmer frame of mind, wouldn't you?

Mental training means preparing yourself for any set of circumstances that may occur on the golf course, so you can cope with them to the best of your golfing ability. Take a situation that is familiar to every golfer. Your ball is lying 60 yards from the flag, with a bunker guarding the green. You know that a simple pitch (the kind you do so well on the practice ground) will drop the ball onto the green, ending up within putting distance of the hole. What happens? You "freeze", and either you hit it short and it lands in the sand, or you increase the length or speed of your swing to make sure that the ball goes over the bunker, and it goes too far, perhaps even into the trees on the other side of the green. You read the situation properly and knew what was required, but you could not get through the bunker-induced mental block, to allow yourself to react automatically and produce the regular swing that would give you a winning shot. You need mental training, just as every good golfer needs it.

Mental training has the advantage over physical training in that you don't have to be on the practice ground to do it. It can, of course, be practised there, but it can also be done at home, on the train or bus, while waiting for an appointment, or wherever you get a few minutes over.

The conscious and subconscious golf mind

Much research has been done on the mind and how it functions – which half controls what, and so on. In this book, we won't try to explain *why* the mind works as it does, but instead, we will concentrate on learning to use the available knowledge of *how* it works, so that we can improve our mental game.

When confronted with something that must be done – for instance, pitching over that bunker onto the green – the conscious mind thinks, while the subconscious mind experiences and remembers that experience. Later on, when you encounter a similar situation, your subconscious remembers what happened and reacts by sending out signals to the body to behave in the same way. If all past experiences of a similar set of circumstances are positive, that is, ended with a successful result, then the subconscious will recall how the body acted to achieve that positive experience the next time it is faced with those circumstances. But if all past experiences of this situation were negative, the subconscious will, unfortunately, react to produce the same experience, the negative. It cannot, of its own accord, change its way of reacting. It must be helped on the way, by being trained.

Your subconscious is a banker

To simplify all this, we can compare the subconscious to a savings-bank account, with a credit column and a debit column. Everything that you experience is deposited into this account, in one or other of the columns. When you add up your credits and debits under a particular golf heading, say "Playing over a greenside bunker", it is important that your credits far outweigh your debits. This is true for everything that happens in your life, and not just for your golfing experiences. But we will concentrate here on what happens to us on the golfing front.

Golfing credits and debits

There is no doubt that, when you hit a successful golf shot, you have a positive experience. A successful golf shot is not hitting that freak 250-yarder, it is playing a shot correctly and within your ability level. Say that your ball is lying well on the fairway, 140 yards from the green. You know that you can reach the green with your no. 6 iron. You pick out your club, play the stroke, and the ball comes to rest on the green. You feel satisfaction – that was a positive experience. This is automatically entered as a credit in your bank account. If you hit the ball badly and have to search for it in the rough, your debit column gets a new entry. If, the next time you are faced with a shot like this, your credit outweighs your debit, then your subconscious will automatically instruct you to react in the way that produced a positive experience, and your chances of reaching the green with the same club are greatly enhanced. The opposite is, of course, true, too. If your bank balance shows that you are in the red, then your chances of visiting the rough again are good.

Increasing your credits

The average golfer will hit the ball between 85 and 105 times during an eighteen-hole round, that is, he or she will have that many shot experiences. On the practice ground, you can increase the number of shot experiences with a single club by concentrating on practising with just that club. There, you are training both physically (your strength,

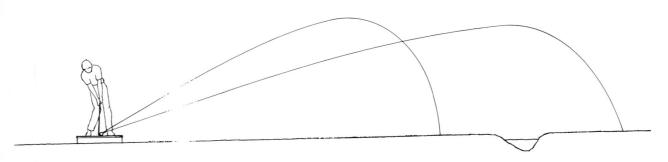

Always play the "honest-to-yourself" shot, which you know is within your capability level. For instance, play the illustrated shot so that you have a good margin to that stream.

If your subconscious knows that you won't hit that long one over the stream, it will probably prove it to you, by seeing to it that the ball ends up in the water.

flexibility, and technique) and mentally (depositing mostly positive experiences, that is, good shots with specified clubs, in your mental bank account.)

However, the most effective mental training is that which you do *without* your clubs, in other words, in your imagination, because you can instruct your imagination to have only positive experiences. That may sound strange, but the interesting thing about the brain is that it is unable to tell the difference between what happens in reality (for instance, when you actually hit the ball with a club) and what you imagine (for instance, when you visualize yourself hitting a shot).

A word of warning is necessary here. Don't try to fool your subconscious. It will only accept an imagined shot if it is actually within your capability. Don't imagine 160-yard fairway shots that land on the green, if you know that, at best, you can hit the ball 110 yards with that club. That is like trying to deposit a rubber cheque as a credit in your mental bank: it will bounce. *Your subconscious knows what you can and can't do.*

Golfer, know thyself!

So, first of all, establish your ability level. You cannot be confident in your game if you are not aware of what you can and cannot do. So, honestly, just how good are you? Being honest with oneself is the beginning of confidence. If, in all honesty, you can say to yourself, "I can hit a drive from this tee so that it lands 170 yards straight down the fairway, 30 yards from that stream," and then actually do it, you are increasing your confidence by confirming your awareness of your ability level, and thus putting another credit in that bank account. If you try to cheat yourself into achieving greater distance with your driver by saying, "I am going to knock this one 210 yards down the fairway over that stream", you are certainly not going to fool your subconscious, because *it knows the truth* about your game. And when you fail to do what you said you would do, your confidence takes a knock, and you have to start all over again to build it up.

Honest knowledge of your swing and its capabilities are vital. Far too many shots are thrown away by trying, for instance, to land a no. 3 iron in a 20-foot area when you

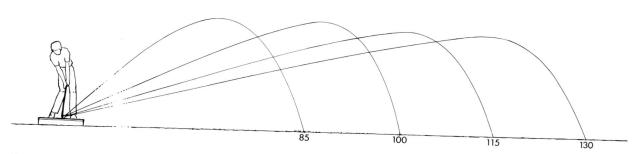

Be sure that you know what your shot-length profile is with each club. Write it up in your notebook, and update it every season or when you notice that your length of shot is changing.

Knowledge of how far you normally hit the ball with each club is a vital part of your mental game.

know quite well that the area of spread of your no. 3 iron is 50 to 80 feet. You are not giving yourself a fair chance if you put extra pressure on yourself to play beyond your ability level, and your shot will therefore finish far worse than if you had played sensibly.

So first and foremost, be honest about your game. Find out how far you can hit the ball with each of your clubs. This means that you are going to have to stand on the practice ground and work out the average distance you hit the ball with each club.

Establish your shot-length profile

Go out on the practice ground first thing in the morning, when nobody else is there and there are no other practice balls lying around to confuse you. Go through your established warming-up routine (see pages 35–37). Then take a club, say the no. 9 iron, and using your normal pre-shot routine and with your full swing, play about twenty practice balls that are in good condition. Play them from a good lie. Then pace the distance to the ball that went straightest and farthest. This is your maximum with the no. 9 iron. Ignore the very worst shots and

try to establish a centre point for the average shots. Note their area of spread. Remember that if the ground is hard, the ball will bounce and roll more than it would do if the ground were soft. Say the average is 90 yards and the balls you use to establish this point lie between 80 and 100 yards. Note this down in your golfing notebook. Don't you have one? Buy one – it is a sound investment. Many golfers feel silly on the practice ground with a little notebook in which they write down what they have done and what results they have achieved, but this is something you are simply going to have to get over, if you are serious about improving your game.

Go through all the clubs in your bag in this way, writing down the average distance you achieved and the area of spread. Tee up the balls for shots with the clubs with which you normally play from a tee. The result is your shot-distance profile. You know now from this exercise that, if you use your no. 9 iron and a full swing, you normally hit the ball 90 yards. You are well on the road to self-knowledge.

Carry out the same exercise from around the green, using your short irons. Establish the length and trajectory of the ball with each of the clubs, noting the length of your backswing and keeping a constant swing speed.

Bring your golfing notebook with you out on the course, and don't be afraid to refer to it when you are actually playing. You now know what realistic target you can pick out when you play with a certain club. And one of the keys to success in your game is knowing your ability level. Knowledge leads to confidence!

The golfing brain

First a word on how your brain works during your round of golf. The brain is composed of two hemispheres, the left and the right hemisphere. You use the left hemisphere to analyze the situation at hand – ball in a good lie on the fairway, 100 yards from the green, sand to the left and rough to the right, wind blowing from behind. The left hemisphere also brings you to the logical conclusion that, with your ability level, you need an 8-iron to reach the green.

The right-hand hemisphere receives this information from the left-hand hemisphere and reacts in an intuitive, artistic way. It makes it possible for you to visualize the successful outcome of your shot before you actually play it and then *allows* you to play the shot automatically (that fluid, "thoughtless" swing which is always the one that produces the best shot).

LEFT-HAND HEMISPHERE ANALYZES THE GOLF SITUATION AND WORKS OUT THE BEST COURSE OF ACTION   **THEN IT COMMUNICATES WITH**   **RIGHT-HAND HEMISPHERE WHICH VISUALIZES THE SUCCESSFUL SHOT, GETS THE RIGHT FEEL AND TEMPO, AND ALLOWS THE BODY TO CARRY OUT THE SWING IN AN EFFORTLESS FLOW.**

To simplify it all, we can say that the left-hand hemisphere is the thinker, and the right-hand hemisphere is the feeler/doer. To play your best golf, it is necessary for both hemispheres to work together. However, they cannot work at the same time. *You cannot think and swing.* So you must be aware of the fact that once the left-hand hemisphere has done its bit and passed on the information to the right-hand side, it should turn off and allow the right-hand side to take over, "feel" the positive result of the shot it visualizes, and then freely "flow" into the effortless swing that will produce that shot.

Using your brain in a golfing situation is like putting on a play. First the play should be one that is likely to be accepted by the public. That is the analysis. (Will the lie of the ball, choice of club, etc. "accept" your shot?) The dress rehearsal gives your imagination a chance to feel the atmosphere and visualize the result required. Your practice swings are the dress rehearsal. And then comes opening night – your actual stroke – in which you automatically and without thinking do exactly the same as you did in dress rehearsal. And the result is — success.

Another way of putting it is to call it C.I.A., that is,

C = Common Sense, which tells you what club to choose and what shot to play.

I = Imagination, which enables you to visualize the successful result of your practice swing.

A = Association, which allows you to repeat your successful practice swing, this time with the ball.

THE FOUR GOLF FUNDAMENTALS

Ever since the game began, golfers have been working to improve their game. Better golf equipment is being produced all the time, more and finer practice areas are being built, and technical aids, such as instruction books, pictures, and video films, are being widely used. Top sportsmen have always been aware of the importance of the proper mental attitude to their sport – only those who combine technical skill with confidence in their own ability to win are able to reach the top – but it was not until the 1970s and 1980s that amateur sportsmen became really aware of the fact that the mind can actually be trained to think positively about winning, and that the sportsmen who trained their minds were those who won the important matches, even though their opponents were technically as skilful as they themselves were.

In the past two decades or so, research in sports psychology – in golf as well as in many other sports – has narrowed down excellence to four fundamentals: knowledge, understanding, technical skill, and the individual's mental attitude. This is especially true of golf.

KNOWLEDGE

In golf, knowledge of the way in which the clubhead strikes the ball is vital for a true understanding of the game. Many expert golf teachers have written about the ball-flight laws, and to refresh our readers' memories and to give them a ready reference guide for their own personal use, we go through these laws briefly.

There are only five factors that affect the flight of the golf ball: the clubhead, the clubhead, the clubhead, the clubhead, and, once again, the clubhead. Now that statement might be considered facetious, but it is meant to make you sit up and pay attention to this very important fact: *all five factors that affect the flight of the ball have to do with the clubhead.* They are:

1. The swing path.
2. The position of the clubface.
3. The angle of approach.
4. The sweet spot.
5. The speed.

SWING PATH

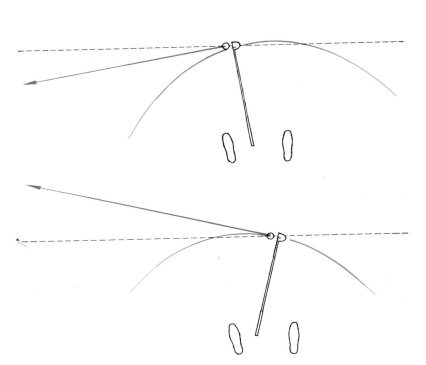

1. IN-TO-ALONG-TO-IN.
The ball starts straight towards
the target.

2. OUT-TO-IN.
The ball starts to the left of the
target.

3. IN-TO-OUT.
The ball starts to the right of the
target.

The swing path

The swing path is the path on which the clubhead is swung. The swing path at impact can be towards the target, to its left, or to its right. The swing path is straight towards the target if, during the downswing, the clubhead moves from the inside of the target line, along it at impact, to move once again to the inside on the follow-through. A downswing started by the shoulders will make the clubhead swing to the left (starting outside and ending inside the target line, that is, out-to-in). Conversely, starting too early from the lower body will cause the clubhead to move to the right of the target, starting inside the target line and continuing outside it (that is, in-to-out). Bad set-up and alignment will also cause an incorrect path.

The swing path, then, dictates the starting direction of the ball. It also affects the angle of approach of the club to the ball.

CLUBFACE DIRECTION AT IMPACT RELEVANT TO SWING PATH

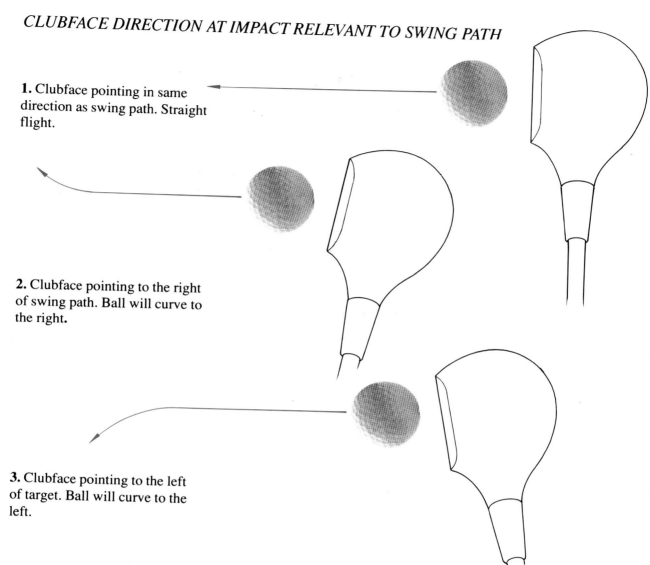

1. Clubface pointing in same direction as swing path. Straight flight.

2. Clubface pointing to the right of swing path. Ball will curve to the right.

3. Clubface pointing to the left of target. Ball will curve to the left.

The position of the clubface

The position of the clubface at impact, i.e, the direction in which the clubface is pointing at impact, is determined by the positioning of the hands on the club and how hard you hold it. At impact, the clubface may be pointing straight at the target, to the left of the target, or to the right of the target. Should the clubface be pointing in the same direction as the swing path, and should both be pointing towards the target, the ball will fly straight towards the target.

If both are pointing the same degree to the left, the ball will fly straight, but to the left. And if both swing path and clubface are pointing the same degree to the right of target, the ball will fly straight, but this time to the right.

If you hit the ball with the clubface pointing in a different direction than the swing path, the ball will curve in the air. Should it curve to the right, a common mistake is to try to compensate this by aiming more to the left, thus changing the swing path. This

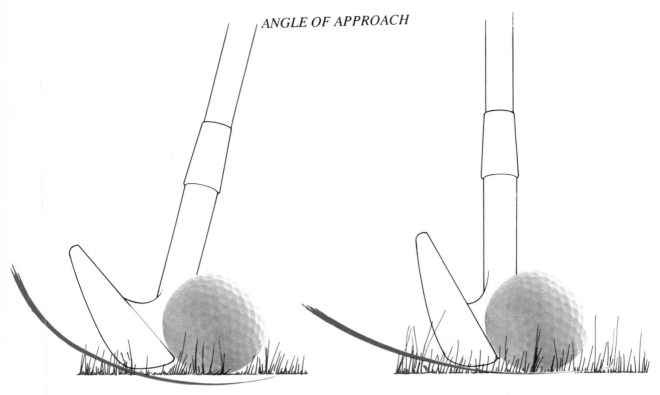

ANGLE OF APPROACH

1. STEEP
This is the angle that you try to achieve with your wedge. The steep angle of approach of the club causes the ball to fly high with backspin.

2. NORMAL (FLATTER)
This is the angle you try to achieve with your no. 3 iron. Very slightly on the downswing at impact. The ball flies longer and lower.

is a natural reaction, but it is totally wrong, because it is the clubface that needs to be changed in order to correct the mistake. If you have the correct clubface position at impact, your chances of swinging the club on the correct swing path will be greatly increased. So remember that the position of the clubface at impact is the most important of the ball-flight laws.

We have now established that the ball will start in the direction you swing the club and finish in the direction the clubface is pointing at impact. So to produce a shot that

flies straight towards your target, you must, at impact, "marry" the position of the clubface to the correct swing path.

The angle of approach
The angle of approach is the angle at which the clubhead comes down to the ball. This affects the height and distance the ball flies. The further you want the ball to fly, the less down and the flatter the arc of the swing should be. The club should approach the ball from inside, behind, and above. For all iron shots, the ball must be struck first, and

THE SWEET SPOT

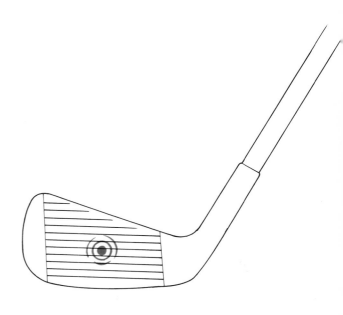

3. SLIGHTLY ON THE UPSWING
This is the angle you try to achieve with the driver off the tee. The ball starts off low and then rises later in its flight.

The sweet spot is individual for each club and is the optimal striking point on the clubface.

the grass second. This is true even for irons off the tee. Wooden clubs off the tee, however, will send the ball further if it is struck slightly on the upswing (just after the lowest part of the swing).

The sweet spot
The sweet spot is the perfect striking point on the clubface. If you do not strike the ball with the sweet spot, but on the toe or the heel, loss of distance and direction will be the result.

Clubhead speed
The speed of the clubhead at impact decides the length of the shot, *if* the other four ball-flight laws are followed.

REMEMBER that no matter how fast you swing the clubhead, if at impact the clubface or swing path is not pointing at the target, the angle of approach is not correct, or the ball is not struck by the clubhead's sweet spot, then your chances of a straight shot with the correct height and length are nil.

BALL-FLIGHT TERMINOLOGY

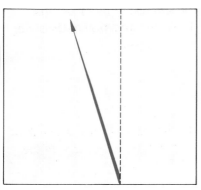

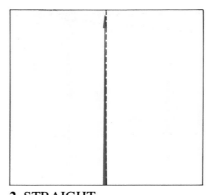

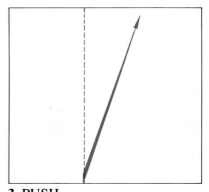

1. PULL
A pull is a shot that starts to the left of the target and continues straight along that path.

2. STRAIGHT
A straight shot is one that starts straight towards the target and continues along that path.

3. PUSH
A push is a shot that starts to the right of the target and continues straight along that path.

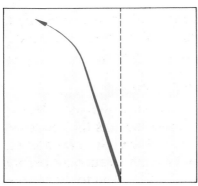

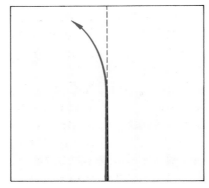

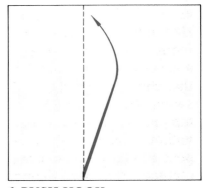

4. PULL-HOOK
A pull-hook is a shot that starts left and curves more left.

5. DRAW
A draw is a shot that starts straight and curves *slightly* left.

6. PUSH-HOOK
A push-hook is a shot that starts right and curves left.

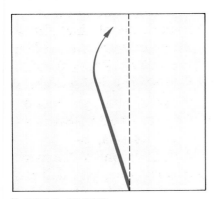

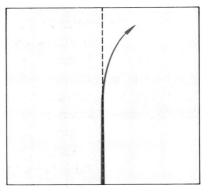

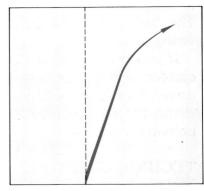

7. PULL-SLICE
A pull-slice is a shot that starts left and curves right.

8. FADE
A fade is a shot that starts straight and curves *slightly* right.

9. PUSH-SLICE
A push-slice is a shot that starts right and then curves more right.

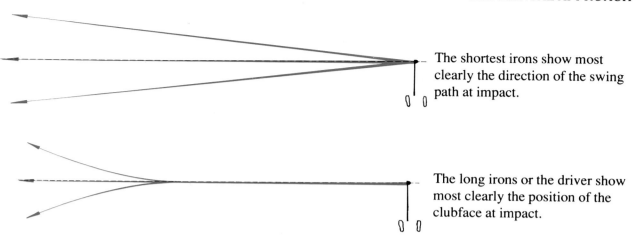

The shortest irons show most clearly the direction of the swing path at impact.

The long irons or the driver show most clearly the position of the clubface at impact.

UNDERSTANDING

With these ball-flight laws firmly in your mind, increase your understanding of your game by practising and playing. Experience will show you the importance of pre-shot routine. It gives you a comfortable feeling of having played the shot before, and besides, it is your set-up and alignment that change the flight of the ball, not your swing. Watch any major tournament. These top players will often fade or draw the ball without changing their swing. What happens is that they alter the position of the clubface by moving their hands on the shaft and changing grip pressure before the swing is set in motion.

If you want to know *the direction* of your swing path at impact, use your short irons. The ball will fly in the direction of the swing path.

If you want to know *the position* of the clubface at impact, use the long irons or the driver. Should the ball curve, it will curve in the direction in which the clubface was pointing at impact.

TECHNICAL SKILL

Technical skill is being able to swing so that the clubface at impact conforms with the ball-flight laws. Players who have good technique can affect the ball flight by changing their set-up and alignment, or by varying hand position and/or finger pressure, in order to produce shots of varying height, curvature, and roll.

Remember that you will benefit most from mental training when your technique is reasonably established, and you have a stable and functioning swing.

MENTAL ATTITUDES

The correct mental attitude will enable you to be *aware* of the situations that arise on the golf course, to *know* your ability level, and to be able to *visualize* your shot before you make it. It will allow you to play more shots by reducing excess nervousness and creating confidence.

Most of the mental blocks we feel are man-made. For instance, think of the four-minute mile. For years, people had aimed at this seemingly invincible barrier. When it was finally conquered, by Roger Bannister, it didn't take very long before others achieved it, too, and nowadays nobody even raises an eyebrow when this once-impossible barrier is broken again.

Once you break through one of the mental blocks in your golf game, you will not be troubled by it again. Mental training will help you to see these blocks for what they are, to relate your ability level to the problem, and to get into the right frame of mind to beat it.

MENTAL TRAINING WITHOUT CLUBS

Try to have your mind-training sessions at the same time of day. Just before going to bed is obviously a good time, because you will be changing into comfortable sleeping wear and the house should be reasonably quiet. Practise for about ten minutes on each occasion, and, as you find it becomes easier, increase the length of each session.

Try to practise regularly. Twice a week to begin with, then daily as you become more proficient.

First of all, relax!
The subconscious is at its most receptive when the mind is in a state of relaxation. And the mind will relax only when the body is relaxed. Don't confuse relaxation with "having a rest". Relaxation is a conscious and deliberate process that you must practise before you can achieve it.

For the beginner, the environment in which you relax is important. Find a peaceful place in your home, where you won't be disturbed. Light is a distraction, so draw the curtains. Wear loose comfortable clothing, and take off your shoes.

Lie down on your back on a mat, a bed, or a sofa. Later on, you can learn to relax even when sitting in a chair.

Methods of relaxing
Start breathing deeply and rhythmically. This will slow down the tempo of your whole body and start the first phase of relaxation. Breathe slowly in through your nose and fill your lungs full, allowing your stomach to distend to take in more air. When your lungs are full, hold your breath for two or three seconds and exhale as slowly as you inhaled, until you feel your abdomen begin to "cave in". Continue at this slow pace. Listen to the sound of your own breathing, and be aware of how your

mind is emptying itself of everything.

The next phase begins when you make a conscious effort to relax your muscles, beginning with the tips of your toes and working upwards, "willing" the different parts of your body to relax. First feel how your toes get heavier and concentrate on this until you have practically no feeling left in them. Then go on and do the same thing with the feet, ankles, calves, knees, thighs, stomach muscles, the small of your back, chest, shoulders, and neck and facial muscles. Roll your eyes up under your closed eyelids; let your mouth open slightly and the lower jaw go slack. Wipe out any tension in the forehead, any frowning. Every single muscle should be relaxed, while your breathing will continue rhythmically, although not as deeply as before. It is now a gentle breathing, in tune with your state of complete mental relaxation. You are ready for a mental training session.

A second method of relaxing the muscles is the tense-and-release method, also known as the Jacobson method. To relax your hand, simply clench it into as tight a fist as you can make. Keep it like that for about five seconds and then release it suddenly. You will notice that the hand's muscles feel soft and relaxed. Do this with each part of your body until you are fully relaxed, with your eyes closed. You do not go to sleep but are in a type of relaxed trance. This is the state in which your subconscious can most easily be influenced.

A third method to help you relax is that which is used by some airlines to calm nervous passengers and is especially useful if you are sitting upright, rather than lying down. Imagine that your body is a vessel, filled to the top with liquid tension. Incidentally, the body is composed of over 70% fluid, so this should not be too diffi-

A MENTAL TRAINING SESSION

1. Relax
Lie or sit comfortably. Deep breathing. Relax your body, part by part.

2. Visualize the problem
Imagine yourself on the course confronted with a particular golfing situation that normally causes you difficulty.

3. Analyze the situation
Consider the lie of the ball, choose your club with reference to the target area and your ability level.

4. Target projection
Go through your pre-shot routine, *see* the flight of the ball in your mind's eye before you play the stroke.

5. Play the stroke
Now play the stroke, feel the perfect swing, and hear the click of solid contact. Watch the successful flight of the ball. Follow it all the way until it has stopped.

6. Enjoy that feeling of success!
You are fully satisfied with the result and a new deposit has been made to your credit in your mental bank account.

7. Repeat
Do this several times to strengthen your muscle memory.

8. "Wake up" slowly
Take a few deep breaths, wriggle your toes and fingers, and get back to normal.

cult! Inhale deeply and, as you exhale, imagine that the liquid is draining out through your toes. As the tension drains from your head, the forehead begins to smoothen out, the eyes relax, then the nose, the sinuses, the cheekbones, the lips, the jaws. Slowly all the tension drains away, as if forced out by your exhaling breath. Breathe like this for a couple of minutes.

Try these exercises, and you will be surprised at how effective they are. Relax like this two or three times a day – a lot of body tension will be released.

Now that you are relaxed, your subconscious is open to receive the messages that you send it. In other words, the mental bank is open and waiting to register any deposits that you want to make on the credit side (or, of course, on the debit side, but you are going to see to it that only credits are made).

Try using the tense-and-release method to relax when you are in any kind of stress situation, either in your everyday life or on the golf course. An example of a stress-filled golfing situation is when you have been kept waiting a couple of minutes before playing a difficult or important shot.

If you have practised relaxing regularly, say every second day for a week or two, you will be able to relax quickly and easily, so that you don't tighten up in difficult situations. Personally, I always have a relaxation session when I come home after a tough day and have a great deal to do, with very little time in which to do it. I lie on the floor and relax completely for just a few minutes and then I get up, refreshed, my mind clear, and can carry on effectively with what I must do.

MASTERING MENTAL BARRIERS

Now that you are relaxed, "send" your mind away from your surroundings. Detach yourself completely from your daily life, its cares and responsibilities. Transport yourself to that place on earth where every golfer should feel happy: the golf course. Don't try to conjure up an imaginary course, but work on a picture of your club course or some other course that you know well. The mind likes that feeling of *déjà vu* and feels at home in familiar surroundings (see page 28). You are now going to take one of your problem situations, that is, the kind of situation that makes you nervous and causes you to lose that automatic swing which invariably gives you a good shot. Many people find playing from the first tee to be particularly problematical. The first tee is often within view of the clubhouse, where all the "experts" are sitting, keeping a critical eye on what is happening and often allowing their comments to be heard. Also, there is usually a queue of players awaiting their turn to start, so the atmosphere is often quite tense, everybody waiting to see if the other player will make a fool of himself.

First-tee nerves

So imagine yourself standing on the first tee, just about to play off. Tee up your ball. Look down the fairway, feel the atmosphere – the people around you who are watching, the birds singing in the trees, and the warmth of the sun. Now look again down the fairway and see in your mind's eye the shot that you are going to play, choose the club, and go through your pre-shot routine. Address the ball, and then play the shot. Feel how your swing flows exactly as you want it to. Hear the sound and feel the strike as the club makes contact with the ball. Continue the swing to a full follow-

through that leaves you in perfect balance. Watch how the ball flies through the air, lands, and then rolls to stop in the target area you have chosen. The shot has taken place exactly as you had imagined. You are completely satisfied. Do this a couple of times every session, making further deposits on the credit side of your mental bank account – and without even swinging a golf club!

Now let your thoughts wander quietly for a minute or two. Think about anything you want to. Then break the spell by taking a few deep breaths, wriggle your fingers and toes, and then move your hands, arms, and legs slightly, until you are completely "awake".

Repeat this session every day, if possible, but at least every second day. Eventually, the credits will outweigh the debits (bad experiences that have occurred in reality on the first tee). This will mean that the psychological block, built up by negative experiences, has been removed by a greater number of positive experiences.

Mental training works!

Now you may react with scepticism when you read the above, and admittedly, it does sound a little like hocus-pocus. But unlike hocus-pocus, this method actually works, as hundreds of top-class golfers, sports psychologists, and golf pros will confirm. Indeed, it is not only in golf that this type of self-suggestion works, it has been used with good results in many other sports and even in business and industry. Try it seriously over a period of, say, three weeks, and you will see for yourself how it works.

Seeing the successful shot in the mind's eye *before* you play (this is known as "visualization" or "target projection") and experiencing the satisfaction of success will

Tension at the first tee. It is not just the player who is feeling nervous. Everyone who is waiting to play is also feeling on edge. Beat this tension and you are making a good start.

develop a pattern of successful actions that will increase your confidence, your enjoyment of the game, and, of course, your chances of winning.

To begin with, treat only one of your golfing problems per session. When you feel that you have that particular problem under control and have proved it in reality by beating it on the course, move on to the next, and treat it in the same way.

Eventually, when you become proficient at this kind of mental training, you will be able to play all eighteen holes of a golf round in this manner, thus making large deposits to your credit in your mental bank account. Playing the eighteen holes mentally several times during the days before a competition is an excellent way of preparing yourself for a successful day.

Hooking into trouble
Another typical problem is a tendency to hook when you have a water hazard on your left, even though your normal swing pro-

duces a straight or slightly sliced shot. Your subconscious cannot accept the word "don't", so if you say, "*Don't* knock it into the water", the only thing it will see is a ball splashing into the water, because your subconscious is only too aware that you are deeply in the red in this matter. Again, mental training sessions with the proper pictures being imagined, will help build up your credit, and you will soon be able to overcome that "hook-into-the-water" syndrome.

However, beware of believing that every golfing problem is the result of some psychological factor or other! This is not necessarily true. It can, for instance, happen that a perfectly good swing deteriorates due to some error in your set-up and alignment, or in your grip. Always discuss golfing problems with your pro to see if the cause is technical or psychological. As stressed earlier, mental training works best when you have a reasonably stable swing technique.

Mental training with clubs

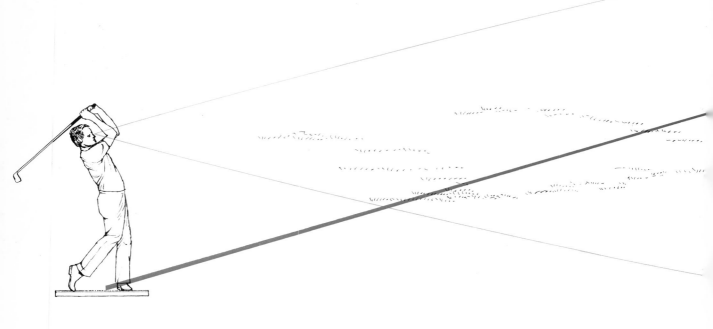

Training target projection on the driving range
Standing on the driving-range mat, you are mentally playing a par-3 hole on the course. In your mind's eye, you are seeing the result of the shot you have not yet taken. This is the way it is going to be, if you play with your normal swing and have not allowed anything extraneous to

Practising on the driving range gives you the opportunity to test your progress with the mental training you have carried out without clubs, as just described. As always before practice, you must warm up, using your established routine (see pages 35–37). If you were working on "first-tee nerves", then you can go out on the driving range and experience in your mind's eye that first-tee situation. Take only one ball from your bucket of practice balls, tee it up, and then look down the driving range, but seeing in your imagination the fairway from the first tee. Feel the atmosphere – the people around you watching, the birds singing in the trees, and the sun shining warmly. Then go through your pre-shot routine, seeing in the mind's eye the shot that you are going to play, how it flies through the air as you planned, lands and then rolls to a stop in the target area. Address the ball and then, in reality, play the shot. Hopefully, it will be as you have visualized. A double credit in your bank account. This success will, of course, greatly increase your confidence, too.

Repeat this with four balls. Take a break, think about what you have achieved, and

cloud your mental vision. Your attention is trained completely on the ball, the path through the air that it will fly, and the landing area on the green. Everything else is blocked out from your concentration. It is the ability to use your imagination to visualize the successful result of the untaken shot that will stand you in good stead when you are playing under pressure.

repeat the exercise three times. Enjoy the success with each shot. Finish the session after this by doing some drills (see page 39), say with your feet together to create good balance, or letting go with your right hand well after impact so as to feel the effect of the clubhead. Remember that even practice should be fun. Finally, play some shots you are particularly good at – this means that you will leave the practice ground with a solid sense of achievement.

When you are next playing a round of golf, test the success of these mind-training sessions. Go confidently up to the first tee, tee up the ball, and look down the fairway. Experience in reality the atmosphere you have previously imagined. Go through your pre-shot routine, see in your mind's eye the ball as it flies perfectly through the air to land and roll to a stop in the planned target area. Address the ball, and then play the shot. Success again. Always take a little time to savour the success before it is deposited in the subconscious.

Mental training, then, consists of two types of training – with and without clubs. Both must be practised to achieve the best effect.

ROUTINE AND DÉJÀ VU

By now, you will have noticed (perhaps with mounting exasperation) that there is a lot of repetition in what we have been saying, and you may have asked yourself, "Why is the author repeating all this about feeling the atmosphere at the first tee and hearing the birds sing? What has this to do with training my mind so that I can play better golf?" The answer is that the repetition is deliberate and that it has everything to do with mental training. The mind feels comfortable when confronted with a situation that it has experienced before (remember that the subconscious cannot tell the difference between what has happened in reality and what has happened in the imagination). That feeling of *déjà vu* puts the mind into what is called a "comfort zone"– it has been there before and the experience was enjoyable. Therefore, you follow a certain pattern in your mind-training sessions, be they with or without golf clubs. Each time you go through a situation, you do it in exactly the same sequence and with the same tempo, thus laying down a pattern that the mind quickly recognizes, automatically instructing the muscles to react in the proper manner. (This helps to create what is known as "muscle memory", which is the reflexive action of groups of muscles when they are instructed by the brain to carry out movements that have been previously performed a sufficient number of times.) The routine sets up that atmosphere of *déjà vu* in which the mind finds itself comfortable and can, therefore, easily recall the necessary instructions to the muscles. The end of this chain of reaction is the successful golf swing.

Concentration

Your mind can be aware of many things at the same time – the fairway, the ball, the club, how you are holding it – but it can concentrate on only one thing at a time. Concentration is the ability to focus all your awareness on a particular object or on something that is happening at just that moment, to the exclusion of all the less relevant objects or happenings around you. It is one of the most important mental skills there is, not only in golf but also in everyday life. When you concentrate fully on a particular golf situation, you do three things: you think in the present tense, you heighten your awareness, and you increase your confidence.

Thinking in the present tense means that you don't think about what has just happened, with your mind still dwelling on that last hole with those three putts ("Quite unnecessary, why didn't I place the ball nearer the hole with my first putt"), or thinking of the hole ahead ("I'd like to get away with a good drive on the next hole") or of the round as a whole ("Out the first nine holes in 38! I can't keep this up – something's going to go badly wrong and bring my score back to normal"). Negative thoughts like this lead only to negative play.

Concentration heightens your awareness by enabling you to disassociate with everything going on around you: things on the outside that are likely to disturb you, such as noise, sudden movements, nervous tension from onlookers, and things on the inside, such as your thoughts – doubt, nervousness, uncertainty, and other feelings.

Because you are not bothered by previous poor play or by fears of obstacles to come, and because your awareness is now sharp, your self-confidence and, therefore, your chances of success increase.

Relaxing physically is the first step towards relaxing mentally. Lying down on a mat or on a bed is helpful in the beginning. Later on, you can learn to relax in many situations – sitting down at home or in the office, in a train or bus, and so on. Once mentally relaxed, you can begin training your mind to concentrate, to target project, and even to play a whole round mentally.

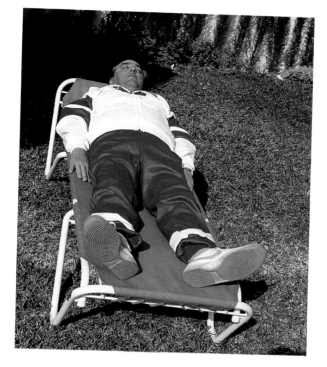

Training your ability to concentrate

You can train your ability to concentrate by simple exercises that you can do almost anywhere. A word of warning: don't try to force yourself to concentrate, that is like forcing yourself to go to sleep – the effect is always the opposite.

How do you learn to induce and control a high level of concentration?

Step 1

Relaxation exercise as on pages 22–23. When you are in a state of relaxation, concentrate your attention on something. For instance, on this book that you are reading. Feel the weight of the book in your hand. Feel the texture of the cover paper and the interaction with your skin. Think about it. Is it cold, warm, soft, hard? When you have answered, you have been concentrating for a few seconds! Try this with some other objects to get used to this way of improving your concentration.

Carry out this exercise several times each day. You will notice that after a few times, you will begin to feel how you are zoning in more and more on the object of your concentration, to the exclusion of everything else about you, and how you can hold that concentration level for longer and longer periods.

Exercising without a club and ball can be done anywhere: on the bus or train, during a coffee break, even in the changing room at the clubhouse. It only takes a few minutes. Deep breathing, relaxation, and total focus on an object is all you need to do. These exercises will, after a few weeks, enable you to use your concentration like you use an electric torch. You switch it on when you need to illuminate an object or a situation – in this case, the golf shot to be played – that demands total mental involvement. You switch it off (to spare the batteries!) when you have played the shot.

Concentrate on the ball only.

Concentrating on the ball and the target area, you see the desired flight from start to finish.

Step 2

The next object you choose to concentrate on should be something that will excite your golf interest, such as a golf ball. Put the ball on the ground, as if you were going to play it. Now relax by the clench-and-release method described earlier (page 22), and look down at the ball, focussing all your attention on it. Look at its shape and colour. Consider its dimples. Think of the way in which your golf swing can make that ball fly perfectly through the air. Do this for thirty seconds at a time. The first thirty seconds always seem the longest. Repeat the exercise five times.

Step 3

Same as Step 2, but now on the practice ground, and with a specific target area involved. Concentrate on the ball first, as it lies on the ground. Then turn your head *slowly* in the direction of the target area. Focus your attention on the target area only, then move your eyes *slowly* back to the ball. Close out all else. Repeat five times, taking a little break in between. During this interval, let your thoughts wander freely.

Club in hand, address the ball. Full concentration on first the ball . . .

and then the ball flight to the target area.

Step 4

Do the same exercise, but this time with a club in your hand. Adopt the address position and hold the club correctly. Now transfer your attention from the club to the ball. Concentrate firstly on the ball, then continue along the desired flight path, finishing on the target area. Repeat five times.

The object of this series of exercises is to increase your concentration, which when you are actually playing should be only on the successful flight, bounce, and roll of the ball, that is, on the "channel" of air through which the ball will fly, and on the target area. It will be as if you have made the light clearer over just these places, while the less relevant parts are covered by a fog or a kind of darkness.

Do these exercises, with or without ball and club, a few times every day.

As your ability to concentrate increases, you will notice that you are able to become absorbed with the situation on hand, so absorbed that there is no room for doubt or fear of failure. The whole swing simply happens, and you are not aware of the details of your swing – the way you hold the club, where the backswing stopped, and so on – but your swing is that wonderful, uncomplicated, and fluid movement that it is when it functions best.

Never try to force your concentration. Like your golf swing, it will only work if you *allow* it to happen.

The importance of practice. Here we have two experienced professionals going through their planned practice session.

CHAPTER 2

PRACTISING

Practice means to repeat something in order to maintain or increase proficiency. To be of true value, your practice sessions must be a planned and leisurely part of your golfing life. It is no good coming out to the practice ground in a hurry, taking a bucket of balls and knocking them into the distance, and then running out onto the course to play. That will not do your golf any good at all. In fact, all you have done is warm up, increase your stress level, lose your tempo, and get into a dither.

PRACTICE MUST BE PLANNED

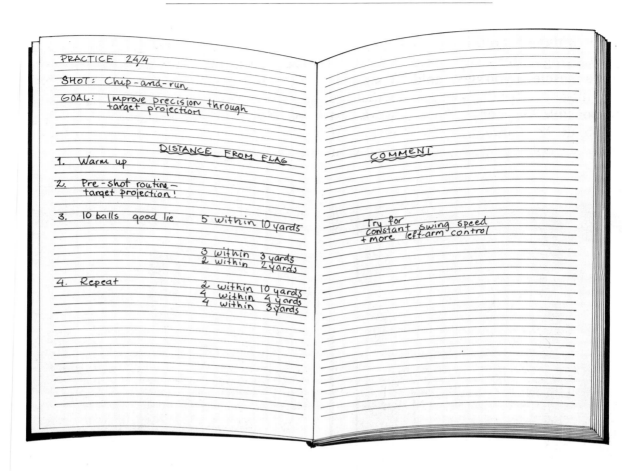

PRACTICE 24/4

SHOT: Chip-and-run

GOAL: Improve precision through target projection

DISTANCE FROM FLAG

1. Warm up

2. Pre-shot routine – target projection!

3. 10 balls good lie — 5 within 10 yards

3 within 3 yards
2 within 2 yards

4. Repeat — 2 within 10 yards
4 within 4 yards
4 within 3 yards

COMMENT

Try for constant swing speed + more left-arm control

Your golf notebook is an invaluable tool for improving your game. In it, you plan your training and note the results, you keep your shot-length profile updated and you note your scores. Keep it small and handy – it should be able to fit neatly into a pocket in your golf bag.

Take your golf practice seriously, and it will give good results. A methodical approach is always best. Recording progress is an important part of your practice. Once again, your invaluable little golfing notebook comes into use.

You will learn more if you come to the golf club *only* to practise, with no intention of playing. Always go out on the practice ground with a clear idea of the part of your game you want to improve during that session. Pick only one thing; more will only confuse matters. Behave before practice as you do when you are going to play a round of golf. Check through your clubs, making sure that you have them all. Go through the same physical warming-up routine that you always use. These actions encourage that *déjà vu* feeling which your mind and muscle memory will respond to without having to try.

WARMING UP

Never start to practise or, for that matter, play, without warming up. Not only will your swing suffer, but you can easily damage a muscle, if you start "cold". Your golfing muscles, that is, the muscles that are responsible for your golf swing, work best at about 98° Fahrenheit (37° Celsius). If they are colder, you will find that your swing will not be smooth and coordinated. Tests have shown that you need to work your golfing muscles hard for five to ten minutes before they reach optimal temperature. The exercises illustrated here are specially designed as a series that will get your golfing muscles well oiled and working smoothly.

Roll your shoulders forwards and backwards fifteen times.

With your arms outstretched from the sides, make small circles in the air. Move your whole arm at the same time. Fifteen times, increasing the size of the circles all the time until you have reached your maximum.

Take your wedge and, with your hands as close together as you can, "dry" your back, as if the club were a towel. Fifteen times.

Write the numbers 1 to 20 in the air with the clubhead. Keep your arm stretched all the time.

Again, write 1 to 20 in the air, but this time with your elbow firmly to your hip.

Finally, write 1 to 20 in the air using only your wrists and hands.

Using a three-quarter swing with your no. 9 iron, hit about ten balls. This will help you to achieve a solid strike at the correct tempo.

Finish your warming-up routine with a dozen or so practice swings aimed at the target, with a suitable interval between each to allow the muscles to return to their normal tension level. Then take a certain number of balls, say ten, and play them with a three-quarter swing with your no. 9 iron, so as to achieve a solid strike with an easy swing at the right tempo, before starting the practice session proper. The object of this pre-practice warming-up session is to create good ball contact with a smooth swing, thus increasing your confidence. Your physical training should never lose sight of the importance of the mental side of your game.

Your practice routine should be exactly the same as the routine you use when actually playing. In other words, *you must practise as you play and play as you practise*. Always use the same pre-shot routine: look at the ball to see what kind of lie it has, look at the target area, choose your intermediate target, go through your regular set-up and alignment routine, visualizing the shot that you are going to play, and then allow it to happen. Stay in the follow-through position, savouring the stroke.

THE PRACTICE SESSION:
Maintaining proficiency

Even though you play regularly you must practise in order to maintain your present standard. If there are no major problems in your game, remember the following.

1. Avoid being a length lunatic. Driver mania is a common golfing disease, so don't use your driver for every single ball in the bucket.

2. Practise mostly your short game: putting and chipping. It is these shots that deteriorate first.

3. Always practise three-quarter swings before full swing movements, and remember to play the full swing movements with the shorter and easier clubs first, but don't funk the difficult ones!

4. Practise shots from rough and bunker.

5. Should you find that you have problems with any particular club, promote confidence by playing a number of balls with a shorter club before returning to the problem club. For example, a no. 5 wood instead of a no. 3 wood, and a no. 4 iron instead of a no. 3 iron.

Practising long shots

Use this session throughout the season to maintain and even increase your level of proficiency. A clear idea of what you want to practise, together with a mental picture of the desired result, is vital. You must also be sure that you can achieve these objectives. Don't try the impossible. First go through the normal warming-up routine, finishing by playing ten shots with a short iron to create a good strike on the ball with a free and easy swing. Only after having succeeded with this, should you start the programme.

1. Choose target and intermediate target. Lay a club on the ground to indicate your swing path through the ball.

2. Place the clubhead behind the ball and align it to the intermediate target.

3. Take your stance, placing first your right foot and then your left. Back fairly straight and knees *slightly* flexed.

4. Alignment routine: feet, knees, hips, shoulders, and eyeline should be parallel to, i.e., slightly to the left of, the target line.

5. In your mind's eye, see the ball flying towards the target, bouncing and rolling to a stop just as you wanted it.

6. When ready, set your swing in motion.

7. Observe the ball flight.

8. Move away after every shot, consider the result, and then go back and start from the beginning. Repeat until you have struck all ten balls.

Take a break and record the result in the notebook. Then pick a new target and repeat.

Don't go on too long. If you get tired, your concentration will be lost and no benefit will be gained. The practice programme just described is suitable for all of your longer shots.

Always finish with a few drills (see below), some shots that you are good at, and a couple of minutes' concentrated putting.

Training throughout the season
Work out a practice programme for the full season and follow it methodically. It should cover all parts of your game. You will find it easier if, every year, you begin with sessions on the green. Compete against yourself in order to make it more interesting and, of course, more fun. Only when you have succeeded in reaching your goal for that distance, should you pass on to longer distances. Therefore, begin by short-putting, to create good movement and also to give you confidence through these simple

successes. Follow up by longer putting before going over to easy chip shots from a good lie. Then, having also achieved success here, say 8 out of 10 chips within four feet of the hole, move further away and practise longer and more difficult chip shots. Next time out, practise easy pitch shots, before progressing in this way to the more difficult pitch and approach shots – and so on until the full game is covered.

This practice programme might, depending on the time you have available, take as much as three weeks. Take the time you need. You cannot practise everything at once, if you want to be successful.

The time spent on each session will depend on your handicap, physical prowess, and powers of concentration.

DRILLS

These are just a few of the drills that will improve your balance, foster the correct swing feeling, and promote greater awareness of swing path and clubface position. Include one or two of these at the end of every practice session to reinforce correct swing feeling and to have some relaxing fun.

1. Swing with your feet together.

2. Swing with your feet together and both heels off the ground throughout the swing.

3. Hit and stop. Stop your follow-through as soon as possible after impact. When the shaft is parallel to

the ground on the follow-through, the toe of the club should be pointing at the sky.

4. Close your stance by putting your right foot further behind your left, to promote a swing from the inside.

5. Place right hand on top of the left with no part of the right hand touching the shaft.

6. Take right hand off shaft well after impact. When you are used to this drill, you can take your hand off progressively earlier after striking the ball.

THE PRACTICE SESSION:
Improvement

Record your practice session in your golf notebook, so that you can keep track of your progress and plan your next session.

It is better to practise correctly three times a week for twenty minutes than to practise once a week for two hours. Don't have a large number of balls in front of you. Hitting two hundred balls badly is not likely to help you improve your golf swing or your scores. Strike a fixed number of balls, say ten, for any particular improvement that you want to work on. Intersperse the shots with practice swings, always relating to your target's distance and direction. Then take a break, sit down, and review the situation objectively. Are you satisfied? Did all the balls fly straight and true, landing rea-sonably close to each other? If not, did they at least all fly in the same direction? Ask yourself what the ball flight tells you about your swing. Go back to the five ball-flight laws that we spoke about in the previous chapter and compare the result of your swing with what they say.

Until you get these laws firmly imprinted in your brain, you should have them written out in your golf notebook, for quick reference. Consult the ball-flight chart shown here, and work out what you have to do to correct your faults.

BALL FLIGHT	WHAT IT TELLS YOU	COMMENTS
Starts straight at target, curves to right at end of flight.	Swing path correct. Clubface incorrect (pointing right, i.e., slightly open at impact).	Move hands to right on shaft and/or relax grip pressure of right hand.
Starts straight at target, curves to left at end of flight.	Swing path correct. Clubface incorrect (pointing left, i.e., slightly closed at impact).	Move hands to left on the shaft and/or increase grip pressure of right hand.
Starts to left of target, curves right; high, short, stops quickly.	Swing path and clubface incorrect. The swing path to the left (out-to-in), and club face points right at impact.	First move hands to right on shaft to straighten ball flight. Then place ball further back in stance to realign body to target. Swing club down from in-to-along-to-in.
Starts to right of target, curves left; low, tends to roll.	Swing path and clubface incorrect. The swing path is to the right (in-to-out); club face points left at impact.	First move hands to left on shaft to straighten ball flight. Then place ball further forward in stance to realign body to target. Clear left hip early on downswing to create an in-to-along-to-in path.
Starts left of target, continues in straight line.	Swing path incorrect (pointing left, i.e., out-to-in). Clubface points in same direction as swing path at impact.	Move ball further back in stance to realign body to target. Swing club down on inside path.
Starts right of target, continues in straight line.	Swing path incorrect (pointing right, i.e., in-to-out). Clubface points in same direction as swing path at impact.	Move ball further forward in stance to realign body to target; clear the left hip at impact.
Starts left of target, curves even more to the left.	Swing path incorrect (pointing left, i.e., out-to-in), clubface at impact pointing even more to left.	Move hands to left on shaft, move ball further back in stance to realign body to target. Swing down on inside path.
Starts right of target, curves even more to the right.	Swing path incorrect (pointing right, i.e., in-to-out). Clubface at impact pointing even more to right.	Move hands to right on shaft. Then move ball further forward to realign body to target. Clear the left hip at impact.
Ball hit thin, halfway up, may fly to left or start left and curve right.	Swing path incorrect (pointing left, i.e., out-to-in), causing angle of approach to be too steep, with upper body too early and club and arms too late at impact.	Swing arms and club freely, down from the inside, with lighter grip pressure.
Ball hit fat, i.e., after clubhead has contacted the ground. Ball flies often to right.	Swing path incorrect (pointing right, i.e., in-to-out), causing angle of approach to be too flat and club to reach ground too early. Lower body is often too still at impact.	Move ball slightly to left in stance to encourage leg and hip movement. Increase pressure in the last 3 fingers of the left hand and the middle 2 of the right hand, and swing through the ball with strong left-side action.

A good swing will strike the ball from the correct angle of approach, with the clubface square to the swing path, which is pointing at the target. These factors are mainly determined by a correct grip, set-up, and alignment, which dictate the flight of the ball before the swing is set in motion.

You will notice that the first adjustments recommended often have to do with the grip, as a correct grip results in a straighter ball flight. The ball flies far more off line when it curves than if it flies straight but in the wrong direction. Once you have the ball flying straight – even if it flies to the left or right – it is easier to correct any other fault. Having got rid of the curve, all you need to do is to move the ball backwards or forwards in the stance to alter the swing path, so that the ball will start along the desired target line.

N.B. It is of great importance that you are on your own, when practising changes, with no disturbing influences to affect your concentration.

Concentrate only on the part of the swing that needs improvement, even when striking the ball. Having done this with the ten balls you have allowed yourself, stop, consider what you have done, and ask yourself if there has been an improvement in your swing and if the ball flight has actually improved, too. (Remember that your new swing will almost certainly feel uncomfortable, and it may take a couple of practice sessions before you actually see an improvement.) Always write down any change of ball flight and swing feeling in your notebook.

If you observe a marked improvement, then back you go again, with another set of balls, and this time swing the club without thinking specifically about what you are trying to correct. Just let the swing happen; then the correction to your movement, whatever it was, will be more easily programmed into your subconscious and your muscle memory.

Should you not be satisfied with your result, consult the ball-flight chart above before starting again.

Remember that the advice of your club professional is invaluable when you have swing problems. Always consult him.

YOUR PRACTICE "SCORE CARD"

As we have pointed out, you cannot practise effectively if you don't keep a record of your progress. To begin with, note the goal of each practice session – say you want to improve the accuracy of your approach shots, remembering how erratic that part of your game was last time you played. Was it your set-up and alignment routine that was wrong? Was your clubface position or swing path incorrect? Or did you just have bad target projection? When you have decided what was wrong, then you plan your campaign. Take your set number of balls, and decide on your target area. Following your usual routine, play them, and then stop, analyze the situation, and make notes.

The following "practice score card" is an example of such a practice session.

DATE: June 7

PRACTICE SESSION GOAL:
Improve the accuracy of 90-yard approach shots.

CLUB: No. 9 iron

NUMBER OF BALLS: 3 X 10

RESULT: Spread of 45 feet around the marker,. seven balls to left and long. Two straight, high, but short. One straight and correct distance.

ANALYSIS: Why were those seven to the left and long? Because the swing path was to the left (from out-to-in), sending ball to the left and also causing the clubface to be slightly less lofted, therefore sending the ball the increased distance. Why were two high and short? Because, in trying to prevent the ball going to the left, the club was held too tightly, preventing the clubface from squaring itself at impact. This open clubface increased the loft, causing the ball to fly higher.

CORRECTIVE ACTION:

1. Check intermediate target. Is it in line with the marker?

2. Check ball position. Ensure that it is not too far forward.

3. Check shoulder alignment. Has it been too far left? Ensure that it is parallel.

4. Check swing for freedom of arm movement up and down and on the inside, using a lighter grip.

5. Play a second series of shots.

This time all balls were straight, seven were perfect, one was topped, and two were hit thinly. The swing path is now correct, but grip pressure is not yet light and constant enough.

6. Write down the result and any changes in swing feel.

Keep these records of your practice so that you can, after a week or two of practising and playing, take a look at what you have done. Has there been an improvement? Have your scores been better? If not, then something is radically wrong, and you must consult your pro once again and ask for advice.

The ultimate goal – your ball drops into the cup.
This is what it's all about!

CHAPTER 3

PUTTING

Of all the strokes in the game of golf, the putt is the one that uses the least physical but the most nervous energy. Having played the long shots well and landed the ball on the green in two, you may very easily have three putts, transporting the ball a fraction of the distance you have just covered with your first two shots. Every golfer has experienced the irony and frustration of this unnecessary situation.

Even though putting well is one of the most difficult parts of the game, too little thought is spent on it and far too little time is spent practising. Indeed, it is very rare for a player to ask his pro for a putting lesson, despite the fact that everyone knows the importance of good putting. In this chapter, we are going to cover a number of putting situations, placing the emphasis on practice. In each situation, we will discuss the right techniques and mental attitudes.

Practise your putting when you have plenty of time, not before you go out to play a round of golf. Don't take more than three or four balls with you onto the green – more may make you lose concentration and become nonchalant.

It is important that you feel comfortable and relaxed when putting. Tenseness, especially in the shoulders or arms, will prevent a free and constant stroke. In the first chapter of this book, you have read about how to control tenseness by deep breathing and the tense-and-release method. Never forget this, it will help you in absolutely every golf situation, and especially in putting.

READING THE GREEN

As you approach the green, examine the way in which it slopes. It is always easier to see this from a distance. Then, as you go around the green to leave your bag in the direction of the next tee, check the slope from the side, with specific attention to the position of your ball and of the hole. (The slope of the green is also known as the borrow.) See in your mind's eye the line that the ball will follow as it rolls towards the hole. Walk along the line, gauging the pace, while clearing away any loose impediments that might cause the ball to go off line.

Don't forget to repair any damage caused by your ball as it landed. If you see marks left by others, repair them, too.

THE PUTTING ROUTINE

Always think in terms of your routine, to establish that familiar and confident feeling of having done it all before. The mind then feels at home with the situation and will allow the stroke to take place in a regular, flowing movement.

Stand a bit behind the ball and view the target line, visualizing how the ball will roll along it to the target. Pick out an intermediate target over which you are going to start the ball on its way to the hole. This can be either a discoloured piece of grass or some faint mark on the ground. Then go and stand beside the ball.

Think first and foremost of becoming comfortable. Each golfer seems to have his own particular putting style, and if your putting is causing you problems, you should examine your target projection, routine, grip, and swing movement. Remember that the grip should discourage any movement of the blade around its own axis.

The reverse overlap grip

The putting grip most used today is called the reverse overlap. Place your hands opposite each other with the thumbs perpendicular down the front of the shaft. The back of your left hand and the palm of your right hand now face the target. Hold the putter lightly with the last three fingers of each hand, then place the left forefinger over the fingers of the right hand.

Practice swings

Before placing the putter behind the ball, take your practice swings. These are a vital part of your pre-shot routine, as they will give you the right feel for the length of swing necessary to make the ball go far enough. Place your club beside the ball and swing it as if you were actually putting, slightly to the inside on the backswing. As you take the swing, feel in your imagination the way in which the ball is struck and visualize it rolling along the target line exactly as you planned. The feeling of success is all-important.

Take this practice swing a couple of times to create the right feel for the amount of movement and speed needed for the ball to reach the target. *Always take the same number of practice swings*. If anything happens to disturb your routine, move away from the ball and then start all over again.

The putt

When you have carried out your practice swings to your satisfaction, address the ball, aiming at the intermediate target. Bend your body forward so that your eyes are over or marginally inside the target line and just behind the ball, giving you a far clearer impression of the line.

Hold the putter with a light grip and your hands over or a little in front of the ball. Swing the club backwards and slightly to the inside, exactly as in your successfully visualized practice swing. Your wrists should be passive so that the club and arms all move in one piece.

Return the clubhead to the ball along the same path that it left it, allowing it to accelerate, but ensuring that the clubhead does not get to the ball before the hands.

It is important to swing the club inside the target line on the backswing, especially with the shorter putts, because it is with these that one tends to take the club straight back, which causes the clubface to close a little, thus sending the ball to the left of the hole.

THE CROSS-HANDED GRIP

Putting is a very personal thing, and on any golf course you will see many different styles and grips used. We have already described the most usual grip, the reverse overlap.

Illustrated here is a grip you might want to use if you have difficulty in keeping the blade of the putter square at impact. It is known as the cross-handed grip and blocks the wrists, thus effectively preventing the blade from turning round the axis of the shaft. It can work wonders, especially for older golfers whose short putting has deteriorated because of uncontrolled and jerky movements. Try for yourself and see if it helps you.

1. In the cross-handed grip, the normal putting grip is reversed, so that your left hand is below the right, but with all fingers on the shaft. This reduces the amount of movement of your wrists, helping you to keep the blade square through the ball.

2. The back of your left hand and the palm of your right hand are pointing towards the target.

THE PUTTING ROUTINE

Whether you use a normal putting grip or some kind of a special grip, such as the cross-handed grip described and used in the following series, *you must always follow the same routine,* as described here.

1. How far from the hole is the ball, how much does the green slope, and in what direction is the grass growing? Pick out the line along which the ball should travel and choose an intermediate target.

2. Take your set number of practice swings and "feel" the length of your shot. Will your swing be sufficient to make sure the ball reaches the target? If yes, go ahead. If no, continue until your practice swing feels right and gives you a mental picture of the successful putt. However, you must get into the habit of always having the same number of practice swings.

3. Address the ball, aim at the intermediate target, and strike the ball with a free, pendulum-like motion of the arms, maintaining the same tempo that you had in the practice swing.

4. *(Opposite)* Keep perfectly still until you have finished the stroke.

STEP-BY-STEP PUTTING

1. Examine the position of the ball with respect to the hole, the borrow of the green, and the direction in which the grass is growing.

2. Stand with the ball between you and the hole, and decide on first the line and then the pace that the ball needs to reach the hole.

3. Pick out an intermediate target — even for short putts. The distance of the intermediate target from the ball depends on the length of the putt, but for a long putt it should preferably be no more than 2 feet away from the ball.

4. Take your practice swings *(always* the same number) and visualize the positive result.

5. Address the ball, aim at the intermediate target, and repeat the swing, striking the ball firmly.

6. Keep still until the ball is well on its way.

THE SHORT PUTT

ther frightened of or not
ut short putts. It is im-
ry putt the same amount
-footer counts as much as
n your score card.

Many ... tts are missed through in-
decisiveness and lack of confidence. When
you are indecisive, you hang over the address position so long that your muscles
"freeze" and when you do hit the ball, the
stroke is jerky, lacking that flow which is
so vital. This is where the importance of an
established putting routine comes in. Your

routine allows you only a certain amount of
time to take in the situation, read the green,
take your practice swings, and address and
strike the ball.

Practise first from a distance no longer
than your putter, and on a flat surface. Place
the balls in a semi-circle round the hole. Go
through the full routine – no shortcuts! –
each time you putt a ball.

When you have achieved success at this
distance, move another foot or so away
from the hole, and repeat the above sequence.

The typical short-putting situation is shown here:
a seemingly simple putt which, if you are not
feeling confident or if you are too nonchalant,
can result in an embarrassing miss.

1. Having stood behind the ball, seen the position
of the hole and the line the successful ball should
follow, pick out the intermediate target. Then
take your practice swings, with enough

movement to put the imaginary ball into the hole.
Visualize the ball rolling into the hole.

2. Then place the clubhead behind the ball,
address the ball, aim at the intermediate target,
and repeat the swing, striking firmly. Keep still
and listen for the sound of the ball rattling into
the cup.

THE MENTAL APPROACH

Lack of confidence ties up with in-decisiveness. Each bad putt, and many bad putts are caused by indecision, makes a debit in the mental bank account. If you have trouble with your short putts, your mental training must concentrate on building up that feeling of confidence through visualizing success-ful short putts and also through actual training on the green, so that you accumulate a nice plus in your mental bank account.

Never practise short putts before a round. Should you miss a couple, you will lose confidence in your short-putting, and your game will suffer.

Always think in terms of your routine, to establish that familiar and confident feeling of having done it all before.

3. Repeat the sequence with the second ball.

4. And again with the third ball. Note the perfectly still body, especially the head. Your ears, not your eyes, should tell you if the putt was successful.

PRACTISING MEDIUM PUTTING

The medium putt is the putt from, say, 6 to 20 feet, and your objective should be either to put the ball in the hole or so close as to make the second putt impossible to miss. More than with the short putt, the medium putt must take account of the slope of the green, the way in which the grass is growing, and even the way in which it is cut. Most weekend golfers tend to hit their medium putts so that the ball either falls short of the hole or falls to the lower side (also called the amateur side). Therefore, it is wise to allow for a little more borrow and distance than you imagine necessary. With the medium putt, direction and distance require the same amount of care – first consider the direction and then the distance.

As always when putting, you must stand absolutely still until the stroke is completed. Practise letting the stroke happen unconsciously, with a free, flowing, yet controlled movement. When you have hit the ball, remain perfectly still. Don't turn your head or body too early.

1. Check the borrow of the green from well behind the ball and preferably from a crouching position. Let your eyes follow the line from the ball to the hole. Remember that the longer and slower a ball rolls, the more it is affected by the borrow.

Clear away any loose impediments from the line.

2. Choose the intermediate target. Take your set number of practice swings and think especially of the length of swing necessary to reach the hole. See in your imagination the ball leave the club, roll along the desired line, and *into* the hole.

THE MENTAL APPROACH

Many high-handicap players miss medium putts because they place too much emphasis on technique (thinking about the mechanics of the swing while making the stroke), instead of using their imagination to visualize the ball being struck on the correct line and with the correct speed.

You cannot think and act at the same time. You have to have the right "feel" for the swing, and, therefore, visualization of success during your practice swings is all-important.

3. Address the ball as usual, aim at your intermediate target, using the same swing as the practice swing, strike the ball, making good, solid contact with the sweet spot, sending the ball along the line into the hole.

4. Now do the same thing with the other practice balls, in exactly the same order. The important thing is to build up a routine that will help you to react consistently each time you are confronted with this kind of situation.

THE LONG PUTT

Any putt over 20 feet from the hole is a long putt. Here, your objective is not necessarily to sink the putt but to leave the ball so near the hole that a second putt will offer no problem.

Greens tend to lean away from high ground, and modern greens are designed to lean towards the front of the green (the edge from which you approach). As you near the green and then walk around it to leave your bag in the direction of the next tee, you will get a good view of the way in which the green is sloping (see also pages 46–47).

The physical side of a successful long putt is to strike the ball at the correct speed. If the green is perfectly flat, the ball will travel in a straight line. It is the borrow of the green that makes the ball curve to the left or right. Good golfers, therefore, play the ball to an imaginary hole which they "see" uphill of the real hole and in a straight line from the ball. The borrow of the slope then takes over and pulls the ball downhill towards the real hole.

In long putting, you want to get the ball as close to the hole as possible, and experience has shown that it is easier to get the line right than the length. Distance is the most important, so when you practise, you should concentrate more on striking the ball consistently at the speed needed to make it roll the right distance. One of the problems with practising long putts is that practice greens are usually quite flat, with very little borrow. It is therefore advisable to try to practise on a "killer" green with very little borrow. It is therefore advisable to try to practise on a "killer" green with lots of borrow, at a time when there are few people on the course. This will sharpen your awareness of both direction and distance.

1. Walk along the line from the ball to the hole, removing any loose impediments, and examining the area around the hole (it is here that the ball will be rolling slowest and therefore will be affected most by any unevenness).

2. Go back to behind the ball, crouch, and check your line once again. Choose your intermediate target, within, say, 2 feet of the ball.

3. Take your set number of practice swings, gauging the speed of clubhead necessary to get the correct distance. Use your imagination to visualize the successful line of the ball and see how the ball stops within the target area.

THE MENTAL APPROACH

You have putted many 30-footers so far in your golf career and in general you have not succeeded in leaving the ball within a 3-foot radius of the hole. Unsureness leads you to under- or overhitting, so that the ball goes no more than halfway to the hole or overshoots it by a good 10 feet. Experience, imagination, "feel", and confidence are the mental qualities that you need to improve your long-distance putting, and this will place less pressure on your other shots.

Experience will help you choose the correct line for a long putt. There is nothing else for it but to practise long putting regularly, so that you build up the ability to read the borrow properly. If one of your fellow players is putting before you, then watch how his ball runs. It may indicate some borrow that you have missed when inspecting the green.

Imagination helps you to translate your experience into "feel". Once you have chosen your line, it is your set number of practice swings, with visualization of the successful result, that will help create the feel for the correct length and speed of your swing movement. Confidence in your ability to carry out what your understanding and imagination have told you, will allow you to create a free and fluid putting movement. It is by mental training both with and without your putter that you build up your putting confidence.

4. Now place the club behind the ball, aiming at the intermediate target, see a successful conclusion, and prepare to play the shot. *Don't* change your mind! Your first decision is usually right, so if you begin to doubt or should you be disturbed in any way, move slowly and quietly away from the ball, and then start again, following the same routine.

5. Now let the shot "happen", strike the ball firmly, and keep still.

6. This time, the ball not only stopped within the target area, but it also ended up in the hole, leaving me with the easiest part of all, picking the ball out of the hole. Another good deposit in the golfing bank!

OFF-GREEN PUTTING:
the foregreen

Accurate putting from the foregreen can dramatically improve your scoring. The reason you should putt rather than chip from the foregreen is that a badly struck chip usually has worse direction and distance than a bad putt. Putting from the foregreen is different from long putting on the green in two ways: you move your weight more forward (to your left foot) and your hands must be more in front of the ball at address and impact. This ensures a more downward strike, eliminating the risk of the putter fastening in the longer grass behind the ball. It also creates a more decisive strike. The ball pops up and rides on top of the longer grass, before rolling smoothly on the green.

PRACTISING FOREGREEN PUTTS

1. Having inspected the lie of the ball, the slope of the green, and the texture of the grass, as usual, you choose your intermediate target. Then take your practice swings to give yourself the right feel for the length of putt required.
Now address the ball. Aim at your intermediate target and check the position of the hole.

2. Striking with the hands in front of the ball will cause it to pop up a little and make it ride on top of the longer grass until it reaches the green.

3. *(Opposite)* Keep perfectly still during the swing, until well after the ball is struck. Repeat for the other balls.

OFF-GREEN PUTTING:
a bare lie

On many golf courses that are heavily trafficked, the area at the sides of the green is often trampled bare, especially in the direction of the next tee. Some people try to chip the ball from here, but the putter is a better choice, because it is far easier to strike the ball correctly from a bare lie with a simple putting movement than by using the hinged-wrist movement associated with pitching.

1. Check the lie of the ball and the position of the flag. Here, the ball is lying tight on the ground, with very little grass. The distance to the near edge of the green is some 20 feet and the pin is about 25 feet further in.

2. Choose your intermediate target. Take your practice swings to get the feel for the right line and distance. When putting from this position, your weight and hands must be more forward than when you putt on the green, in order to eliminate the risk of catching the ground behind the ball.

THE MENTAL APPROACH

Only through regular practice will you have acquired enough experience to be aware that the correct shot to play here is a putt.

Many golfers feel embarrassed putting in a situation like this, but this is completely unnecessary, as professionals always choose the shot that gives them the best chance of success.

The fact that you chose the putter instead of the pitching wedge or sand iron shows that you are already well on your way to becoming a better golfer.

3. Place the club behind the ball, aiming at the intermediate target. Check the line to the hole. Your hands and weight are to the left.

4. Play the stroke, repeating your practice swing. Your hands pass freely through the hitting area, sending the ball bouncing up the slope and onto the green, where it rolls to the flag, leaving you with a simple putt.

OFF-GREEN PUTTING:
a side-slope lie

1. This is pretty much the same situation as that just discussed, but you now have the ball lying on a side slope and uphill. Check the line. Here it is necessary to start the ball well to the right of the hole, to offset the effect of the slope, so the intermediate target is well to the right of the straight line between the ball and the hole.

2. Stance is very important when putting from this position. Stand with your feet square to the line between your ball and the intermediate target.

3. Take your practice swings, and, as always when putting from outside the green, with your hands and your weight more to the left. Visualize the roll of the ball, ensuring that your swing is sufficiently long to speed the ball over the rough ground, onto the green, stopping near the flag.

4. Now place the clubhead behind the ball, in line with your intermediate target, and check the line again, before allowing yourself to imitate the successful practice swing and strike the ball. In the illustrated situation, the ball starts off to the right, and then bounces up the side slope, where it curves to the left before rolling onto the green, stopping by the hole. Another increase on the credit column in your bank account!

OFF-GREEN PUTTING:
down the slope

Here the fast, sloping green has been missed and the ball has finished to the right, leaving a delicate shot to be played down the incline, over the rising foregreen, to stop on the down slope by the flag.

Should you choose to pitch the ball, and it lands short and on the incline, it is sure to bounce forward and roll off the green on the other side. If you pitch it just short, but onto the level foregreen, it will stop immediately. The landing area for a success-ful shot is probably too small for all but the brave or foolish – the green slopes away from us some 8 feet short of the flag, making it very difficult to make a pitch shot stop near the hole. Therefore, why not consider the putter? All that is necessary is to give the ball sufficient speed to roll it down the incline onto the green where it will roll gently towards the hole, with very little risk of overshooting the target.

1. Check the desired line very carefully, as there is also a side slope to be taken into consideration. So your intermediate target must be chosen with extra care.

2. Stand comfortably with the right knee more bent than usual to offset the steepness of the incline.

3. *(Opposite)* Take your practice swings, as usual, to gain an absolutely clear picture in your mind as to how the ball will roll down the slope, gently onto the green, and slowly towards the flag.

A correctly visualized and executed chip from
here will leave you with a simple putt.

CHAPTER 4

THINK RIGHT, CHIP WELL

The chip is the shot that has minimum air time and maximum ground time. The ball is up in the air as little and as low as possible, lands on the green, and then rolls to the target. It can be played with any club from a no. 4 iron to a wedge, the choice of club depending on the lie of the ball, how far you want the ball to travel in the air, and how far you want it to roll after landing. A more lofted club will send the ball higher in the air with less roll after landing.

Some people say that the chipped ball should be in the air one-third and roll two-thirds of the distance. This is not necessarily true, as it depends on the lie, how far you are from the edge of the green, and the distance from the edge of the green to the flag. Other factors that affect the shot to be played will be the speed and slope of the green.

Choosing the club
Choose a club with more loft than you would first think necessary. The reason for this is that the correct chipping stance will de-loft your club, which could give you the feeling that you are not going to get enough height. To counteract this, you may try to scoop the ball into the air, and this will have disastrous results.

If you wish to play onto the green from 10 to 15 feet, don't try to land the ball on the first 5 or 6 inches of the green. Always allow a margin of error to make sure the ball actually lands on the green. An aircraft coming in to land does not touch down just inside the airport perimeter; the pilot clears the perimeter with plenty of margin, giving the aircraft lots of room to come down and roll to a stop. The longer the runway, the safer it is. Always play safe with your chip.

The chipping position

The correct chipping position is with the stance slightly open (left foot pulled back from the line), and the toes, knees, and hips turned a little towards the target, shoulders square, and with your weight on the left foot. The ball should be back of centre and the hands well in front of the ball. This helps you to swing the club so as to strike the ball a descending blow. Other than this, the chip shot is a copy of the normal putt.

The swing

The chip is primarily a one-piece arm movement, with the elbows the same distance from each other throughout. The movement can be compared to the swinging of a pendulum, except that the backswing will be slightly higher than the follow-through, because more weight is on the left foot.

Having played the shot, remain still until the ball has actually stopped. This may seem a little peculiar, but doing this will quickly teach you how much swing movement you need to get the ball to cover a certain distance. Remaining in the finish position until the ball has stopped will teach you feeling for distance and sharpen your muscle memory. If you leave this position too early, you will not learn anything beneficial from playing the shot. Later, when confronted with a similar shot, you will have no memory of the length and speed needed to reproduce the stroke.

Even though the chip is a relatively short shot, visualizing a successful result beforehand is very important. Even the easier shots from around the green require this target projection. Don't be one of those who play the difficult chips well, only to miss the simple ones by not taking practice swings and using target projection. Give even the simplest shots around the green their due respect and your ball will finish at the hole – or why not in it?

THE SIMPLE CHIP

This is one of the shots where you need the ultimate in precision, because the ball must finish in or very near the hole. A good chip from this position can save you a stroke. Normally, if your ball is on the green, some way from the flag, two putts are acceptable, but just because your ball is off the putting surface does not mean that you still need two putts. You should be able to chip it easily to the flag, leaving you with a simple putt.

The possibility of sinking the simple chip and the need for precision mentioned above, often unsettles a player, causing the swing movement to be nervous and jerky. And because it is an "easy" shot, you are expected to play it well, which only adds to the pressure.

To beat this, you must have a clear mental picture of how the ball will behave, both in the air and during its roll. This, together with your pre-shot routine, will reduce the tension in the situation, allowing you to concentrate on a successful shot. Anybody who can play these simple shots well will save many strokes and defeat players who have a much better longer game – much to the long-hitter's surprise and annoyance.

PRACTISING THE SIMPLE CHIP

1. Study the lie, the distance to the landing spot, and the length of roll to the hole. The flag is quite close and this particular green is very fast, so the club chosen is a no. 8 iron.

2. Hands lower down on the shaft and in front of the ball, weight more on left foot, stance slightly open. Take some practice swings until you can visualize a successful result.

3. Place the clubhead behind the ball. Aim exactly at your intermediate target, checking the landing spot and hole for distance before taking your position.

4. Play the shot as an exact copy of your successful practice swing, remaining quite still *until the ball has stopped*. Repeat the full routine with the other balls.

THE SIMPLE CHIP IN PLAY

Regular practice has made your chip swing so automatic that, without thinking, you adapt your swing movement to the height and length of shot required, so when you come to this kind of situation in a game, you simply follow your established routine.

Here, the ball is 10 feet short of the green and another 20 to the flag, so the simple chip just practised is the correct shot to play. Although this is an "easy" shot, you must, as always, use target projection, and it may be difficult to concentrate on visualizing if you are nonchalant or if the stroke is important and you are too nervous.

1. Examine the lie of the ball, then walk along the line, to decide the distance the ball should be in the air before landing with sufficient margin to carry the foregreen. Choose a club with enough loft to provide the necessary flight and roll.

2. Adopt the normal chipping stance and take your practice swings, visualizing as always the successful result of the shot to achieve the right feel for the movement.

3. Place the clubhead behind the ball, aiming at your intermediate target, looking frequently at your landing spot, and creating good target projection.

4. Play the shot, allowing the club to swing freely and exactly as in the successful practice swing.

5. Stand still until the ball stops, savouring the satisfaction that a stroke-saving chip will give. This will build up your confidence and enable you to approach this shot with assurance next time you are faced with it.

CHIPPING UPHILL ONTO A RIGHT-TO-LEFT SLOPE

The ball is lying on the foregreen, 6 feet from the green, and the flag is all of 70 feet up the slope, which also leans from right to left. The ball must fly low to create the speed to roll far enough up the bank before curving left towards the flag. The danger here is that you will try to hit the ball hard to get it to travel the full distance, rather than allow your awareness of your swing's capabilities take command.

THE MENTAL APPROACH

Cool appraisal of the situation, visualizing the flight and roll of the successful shot, and using your established routine are what you need to do to prepare yourself mentally for this shot.

1. Examine the lie of the ball and then walk up to the flag to gauge the slope and the distance.

2. Taking into consideration the distance and the uphill path, choose the club. Here, a no. 4 iron is best. Pick out your intermediate target, which, on this slope, must be to the right of the flag.

3. Take your practice swings, visualizing the bounce, roll, and right-to-left curve of the ball. Once you feel that you have achieved the correct practice swing, address the ball.

4. Play the shot, repeating that successful practice swing. The ball flies low over the intermediate target.

5. Here we see it still in the air before landing at the chosen spot, 15 feet into the green, then ...

6. ... rolling uphill and curving to the left, to stop 3 feet short, leaving an uphill putt. Savour that shot. That's how you are going to do it next time, too.

CHIPPING DOWNHILL ONTO A LEFT-TO-RIGHT SLOPE

Chipping downhill is scary, because of the danger of the ball rolling too far past the hole. The ball here is lying 5 feet short of the green on an up-slope, with the flag 25 feet downhill and on a left-to-right slope.

The ball must be in the air high and far enough to the left, so that, on landing, it rolls gently down the slope, stopping just below the hole, leaving a simple, uphill putt.

1. Having picked the line and walked to the flag to gauge the distance required, select the club. Here, because the ball is lying well and on an up-slope, the no. 7 iron is your choice.

2. Take your practice swings, seeing the perfect flight, bounce, and roll of the ball.

3. Place the clubhead behind the ball, square to the intermediate target.

4. Play the shot over the intermediate target, well to the left of the flag.

5. The ball has landed on the chosen spot, rolled downhill, curving from left to right, to stop just past the flag. You now have a short uphill putt.

SCRAMBLING UP THE BANK

1. To bounce a ball up a foregreen slope is the only way to place it near the hole, if the flag is close to the edge of the green. A chip, or even a pitch, that landed on the green would roll too far past the hole, leaving too long a putt. You have a problem here, and the best way out of it is to "scramble" the ball up the bank with a low, punch-like shot, keeping your hands firm and striking decisively. All this runs through your head as you stand behind the ball and pick out your line of attack.

The ball is lying lower than the green and 20 feet from the edge.

2. Your pre-shot routine is as usual for a chip shot, but the club you choose is longer than you would normally choose for this distance. Take some practice swings until you feel that you have the right movement required for this firm stroke. Visualize the successful flight, bounce, and roll of the ball.

3. Take up the address position, remembering to keep your hands firmly on the shaft and in front of the ball.

4. Keeping the upper body quite still to ensure correct contact, strike low and decisively, aware that it is better that the ball stop past the flag than just short of the flag and still on the foregreen.
The ball leaves the clubhead at a low trajectory, bouncing soon before scrambling up the bank to roll onto the green.

Target projection and proper set-up and
alignment prepare the way for a good approach
shot.

CHAPTER FIVE

HOW TO APPROACH APPROACH SHOTS

The object of the approach shot is to put the ball on the green, as near the flag as possible, and you normally use the short irons for this. The short irons are precision clubs and produce the best results when you concentrate on accuracy rather than length. This can cause middle- and high-handicap players some problems, because they tend to choose *too* short a club and go for length, and this always results in poor accuracy.

Elite players hit the ball farther than middle and high handicappers, but it is noticeable that when they play approach shots onto the green from, say, 135 yards, they take a no. 7 or a no. 8 iron, while the high handicapper tends to choose the no. 9 iron or the wedges and then tries to hit the ball with full power, and often ends up with the ball off the green, for instance in a left-hand greenside bunker.

THE HIGH, SOFT PITCH

This is your third shot on a par 5 hole. The ball is lying well, slightly above your feet, 40 yards from the flag, with the end of a bunker blocking the way. As the green itself stretches well to the right, you could hit a low chip shot well to the right of the flag, giving yourself at least two putts to get the ball in the hole on par. But a well-placed high pitch can give you an easy short putt for a birdie. What will you do?

Make an honest analysis of your chances with a pitch that will arc over the corner of the bunker and land the ball softly near the flag. Knowing that you are capable of this basically simple shot if you can use your imagination for successful target projection and your practice swings to get the right feel for the length of the swing required, you go for the high pitch. A positive and confident attitude of mind will be built up by your visualization, and if you find yourself tightening up at the thought of that bunker and a lost par, don't forget to relax with some deep breathing and loosening-up exercises before starting the visualization process again.

Club selection is no problem from a lie like this: the pitching wedge or the sand iron are the alternatives; they have the loft necessary to give the ball a high trajectory over the bunker and to land it on the green softly, in order to avoid excessive roll. The lie of the ball is good, and the only problem is psychological – the picture of the nightmare mis-hit that will trickle the ball into that bunker.

1. Prepare to take your practice swings. Don't rush, but get yourself into a relaxed and confident mood. Take time over your grip. The club should be held lower down on the shaft to narrow the arc, and with both hands slightly turned to the left to create height. Pick out your intermediate target.

2. Take your practice swing, with your weight favouring your right foot, your hands above the ball, and the ball a little forward in the stance. Break the wrists early on the backswing. A half-swing is sufficient for this distance, and remember that softness is the essence of this shot.

THE MENTAL APPROACH

This is the kind of situation where imagination and confidence are the vital mental requirements; imagination to take care of target projection, and confidence (a solid credit in that mental bank account you have built up during mental training sessions) to allow you to repeat your successful practice swings during the actual shot.

Experience will tell you how long the backswing must be in order to achieve

the distance necessary. The only way to get experience is to practise, learning how far the ball will travel for each length of backswing you take.

Take several practice swings to build up the feel for the distance necessary. Naturally, if you are not sure that the practice swing has the necessary length or pace, then repeat until you are satisfied.

3. The soft, slow downswing should continue through the hitting area, with the left hand and arm leading back to the address position, preventing the club from closing too early. Finish the practice swing with a high follow-through. Feel how you are in balance and visualize the perfect stroke.

4. The moment of truth – your actual shot. This is a repeat of the practice swings that you saw finish so well. Just let it happen, and your muscle memory will produce a free and unhurried swing.

THE SHORT PITCH OVER A BUNKER

Everybody, even the professionals, can feel anxiety in this situation. The problem with a shot like this is that you are afraid that you are not going to get the necessary height to clear the bunker. You either exaggerate the length of the backswing and hit the ball too far, or you try to lift the ball and strike it fat or thin, i.e., hit the ground first or top the ball, both with disastrous results.

The solution is good target projection during your practice swings. Hold the club well down the shaft, pick out your intermediate target, take your practice swings as usual, judging the amount of backswing required. With firm and constant hand pressure and a swing that comes mainly from the arms, you swing with a solid downward blow, to make sharp and distinct contact with the ball, giving it the backspin that causes it to brake quickly after landing. Hold the club lower and firmer, thus reducing the amount of wrist movement and shortening your backswing. This enables you to strike the ball with the necessary authority.

THE MENTAL APPROACH

When faced with a shot over a bunker, you must call upon all the credit that you have in your mental bank account so that your imagination will not be blocked from seeing clear pictures of a successful shot when you take your practice swings.

Remember, too, that you must remain quite still until the ball is well on its way. The temptation is to look up too early, and without target projection it is easy to do this, thus ruining your shot.

1. Practice swing to create target projection and feel. Hands well down on the shaft.

2. The actual swing is, as usual, a repetition of your successful practice swing. Here, the backswing.

3. Nearing the finish of the swing, your weight is planted on the left heel and the right heel is slightly raised. The left hand and arm are still leading the clubhead, as they were during the downswing, so that the ball was struck while the club was still descending.

THE APPROACH SHOT WITH A NO. 8 OR 9 IRON

Here, the ball is 110 yards from the green and there is another 10 yards to the flag. A small valley in between hides some dead ground, and this always tends to make the distance seem shorter. A bunker guards the right side of the green, but as the flag is well back and the green slopes from left to right, it should not come into play. The green is elevated, so everything suggests a full swing movement, with sufficient club to carry well onto the left of the green, away from the bunker on the right, and after bouncing, rolling towards the hole.

1. Study the lie and the distance to the flag. Decide on the club. Visualize the successful flight of the ball and how it bounces and rolls towards the flag.

2. Knowing how far you want the ball to fly in the air and how it should behave on landing, your practice swings will create the movement you feel necessary. Visualize the successful result.

THE MENTAL APPROACH

Even though this is a fairly straightforward shot, awareness is necessary, to avoid the common mistake of not taking into consideration the dead ground and the elevated green when choosing the club. A full swing movement with the correct club will not only keep the ball away from that bunker but will land it well into the green.

3. Hit the ball with the same swing as the successful practice swing.

4. Remain still until the ball is well on its way. Here, we see it on the green, rolling down to the right towards the flag. Another good deposit in the mental bank account.

THE WEDGE SHOT

This particular situation is one that causes many golfers unnecessary anxiety. It shouldn't, because the ball is lying well, and the bunker is actually a help, as in this case it acts as a distance marker, making it easier for you to see the imagined flight of the ball. The ball is 80 yards from the hole, so if you strike it with sufficient movement to carry the bunker with a little margin, you will give it enough backspin to make it stop quickly after landing.

THE MENTAL APPROACH

People are frightened of this shot, as they all too often foresee a negative result, with the ball buried in the sand. Therefore, target projection must not only leave you with a clear picture of a successful shot, but also create feeling for the length of swing necessary.

Practise this shot from different distances, until you have acquired the right feeling for the length of backswing needed to send the ball the given distances. The object is to program your muscle memory to produce the correct swing when faced with these distances on the course.

1. Choose your intermediate target and carry out your pre-shot routine. Ball in the middle of the stance, weight centred, hands in front of the ball. Take your practice swings until you find one with the right amount of movement for this shot, visualizing all the while the perfect result.

2. Play the stroke. The backswing will be about shoulder-high. In fact, the wedge shot from this distance is very similar to your normal swing movement.

3. *(Opposite)* Swinging freely downwards to strike the ball first and the ground afterwards allows the loft of the club to do the work. No attempt should be made to assist the club, as the position of the ball, your address, and swing movement are all that is needed to fly the ball high and far enough.

THE SHORT IRONS ONTO THE GREEN

You played your 125-yard approach shot with the no. 8 iron, but despite a good strike, the ball lands 10 yards short of the green and stops on the second bounce, leaving you with an unnecessarily difficult chip or a very long putt. The swing was correctly executed and the ball was struck well, so why did the ball fall short? The answer is either that you are still not aware of your shot-length profile (see page 13) or that you misjudged the distance. But whatever the answer, you chose the wrong club. Remember that your short irons are for putting the ball onto the green and close to the flag, not just anywhere near the green. If you play your short-iron shot as if you intended it to land in the hole, it will finish near the flag, as these shots tend to have lots of backspin that will stop the ball quickly. So you need a fair bit of courage and confidence to be successful with these shots.

You should have chosen your no. 7 iron for this shot. Use this information to increase your awareness of your shot-length profile, and don't forget to work on your profile for your short irons when you are practising. Next time you have a similar approach shot to play, do the following.

1. Taking your no. 7 iron, you stand behind the ball, picking out your intermediate target and seeing a successful result in your mind's eye. Your intention with this shot is to put the ball not only on the green but near the flag.

2. Set-up and alignment are normal. Keep your weight centred. Hands and shaft must be in a straight line. Your head must be behind the ball and your right arm relaxed.

3. At the top of the backswing, the club is not quite horizontal, and you can see the weight being transferred onto the left foot, to pull the clubhead down to the ball from the inside.

THE MENTAL APPROACH

Awareness of your own ability is most important when approaching the green with a shot like this. Build up your confidence by practising with your short irons and keeping your shot-length profile up-to-date.

A good drive has landed the ball perfectly on the
fairway, offering a chance to hit the green on this
par-5 hole with the second shot.

CHAPTER 6

ON THE FAIRWAY

There are no good or bad holes on a golf course, only holes yet to be played. There are, however, certain holes that can be unsettling, simply because you have played them badly before. If you make three double-bogeys in succession on the same hole, you just know that you are going to do it again the fourth time – and of course you do. Your mental bank account for this hole shows a hefty deficit! You must turn that account from red to black. So if a certain hole has become your "problem" hole, take several balls and play the hole in different ways, on a day when the course is not too busy. Experiment with different clubs until you have found the correct way for you to play the hole. Good practice shots at this hole will rid you of the bad mental picture and build up your confidence. Then the next time you play, the hole will be just another golf hole, and your credit rating will be tops.

The following four pages show a par-5 hole with a second shot that can be played in a number of ways. There is a stream in between the ball and the green, and the question is, should you try to carry the stream with your no. 3 wood or take a no. 4 iron and leave yourself with a longer, but perhaps easier, third shot over the water? A complicating factor is that your first shot has left you with a slightly uphill and side-hill lie. An uphill lie tends to result in a draw, and this side-hill lie tends to cause a fade, so they balance each other out.

Should you feel that the distance required to give you any chance at all of carrying the stream in two, with the opportunity of a birdie, requires the use of the driver from the tee, then it is the second shot that must be practised. Up until now, it is this shot that has caused the problem, as it has almost always ended up in the water.

Assuming that you have played your normal drive, go to the area where it would have landed, and plan how to beat the hole from there. Take a number of practice balls with you and play a series of shots with different clubs until you have achieved the result you can expect with your ability. Remember that you are not interested in freak shots, but in shots that are typical of your shot-length profile and handicap.

PRACTISING TO BEAT THAT PROBLEM HOLE:
with the no. 3 wood

To ascertain if it is actually possible to reach the green from here with your second shot, tee up two balls and play them, noting the result.

Thereafter, play a couple more from a mediocre lie with the same club, and compare the results. Did any balls reach the green? Did all of them carry the stream with sufficient margin of error, leaving a simple approach shot? Or did they end up in the

1. Ball teed up, checking the intermediate target, and "seeing" the desired flight of ball to the finish.

2. Set-up and alignment routine as always, ensuring the clubface is pointing at the intermediate target. Then play the shot and note the result. Tee up another ball, and do it again, following your normal routine.

water, as they always seem to do on this particular problem hole? The answers to these questions establish your shot-length ability and increase your awareness of the situation, both being important steps on the way to success.

3. Now, from the same place, a full backswing with the no. 3 wood, this time with the ball from a mediocre lie, *not* teed up.

4. Free arm swing through the ball, to a full, balanced finish.
 Repeat this from the same lie and check the result. Note it in your notebook.

PRACTISING TO BEAT THAT PROBLEM HOLE:
with the no. 4 iron

1. Set-up and alignment routine, imagining the flight of the ball.

2. Backswing completed.

3. Through the ball, arms flowing out.

4. Ending in a full, well-balanced finish, and savouring the result.

Again, note the results of these shots in your notebook.

THE MENTAL APPROACH

You have now increased your awareness of what you can expect to achieve from this position with different clubs. In this case, nothing was gained by taking the no. 3 wood, so in future, you will automatically choose the club that gave you the best result, the no. 4 iron. The success of the no. 4 iron is a healthy credit in your mental bank account, and this will rid you of the anxiety that this hole caused you. Instead of anxiety, you will feel confidence, when faced with this shot again.

THINKING CLEARLY

Time for thinking clearly on the golf course is often very short. There might be a lot of traffic on the course, or the others in your ball may not be giving you any time to analyze the situation before you take your shot. But it is important that you learn the knack of finding those few seconds where you can concentrate on the lie of your ball, distance to the flag, and all the other factors that will influence your shot. Thinking clearly will save strokes. Take, for instance, the following situation.

The ball to be played lies about 230 yards from the green and very slightly downhill.

The dangers are obvious, and the greatest one is the bunker to the right, 70 yards short of the green. Knowing that you are not going to be able to reach the green with this shot, you must plan what target will give you the easiest possible following shot onto the green. What decision should you make about choice of club and type of shot to play?

What are your options?
1) Hit it straight over the right-hand bunker. However, if you mis-hit, your next shot might be very difficult indeed.

1. Aware of the fact that the downhill lie will encourage a fade, a normal grip on the club and an intermediate target in line with the centre of the greenside bunker will be perfect.

2. Ready to go, everything aligned with the left-hand bunker.

3. *(Opposite)* The ball starts on the desired line, before fading nicely to the right, leaving an easy pitch for a birdie chance.

2) Play left and leave the ball short of the left-hand greenside bunker. This is a better idea, but the flag is near the front of the green and placed well to the right. Not much room to work with here.

3) The third possibility is the correct answer: a slight fade with the ball starting down the left-hand side of the fairway and falling away to the right. A slightly open clubface to offset the downhill lie will create added height and fade the ball. To get well past that bunker, you will need a wooden club, and you know that your no.

3 will do the job with a good margin. This should leave an easy pitch, with plenty of green to the left of the flag, and that is a much simpler shot than a delicate wedge over the left-hand bunker.

THE RIGHT CHOICE OF CLUB:
tee shot

Choosing the right club is vital, and if you can learn to think clearly and choose right, then your chances of success are greater.

On the following four pages we follow a hole from tee to green to show why the clubs were chosen for just those strokes. The right choice of club depends on a number of factors:

1. Standing on the fourth tee, the marker tells you that the hole is a par-4 dog-leg right with a fairway bunker. The hole is 348 metres (380 yards) from the tee. The fairway bunker lies downhill and 250 yards from the tee, which today you might possibly reach with your driver. To be certain of playing short of the bunker, you choose your no. 3 wood.

2. Tee the ball, look down the fairway at your target area, which is safely short of the bunker. Have you given yourself sufficient margin? Are you absolutely sure that you cannot reach the hazard, even if you strike the ball better than normal?

1) How well you are playing on the day. Are you striking the ball well? *Remember that you don't achieve your maximum distance every time you strike the ball.*

2) The lie of the ball.

3) The distance to the target, taking into account weather and wind.

4) Are you playing up- or downhill?

5) What hazards are in your path?

3. Pre-shot routine as usual, placing the clubhead behind the ball and aiming at your intermediate target first. Note how the ball is teed lower than when using the driver.

4. Quite certain in your mind of the direction and distance the ball will travel, you can now allow the swing to take place as usual.

(The second shot on this hole is discussed overleaf))

THE RIGHT CHOICE OF CLUB:
second shot

The tee shot was successful, and now the ball is lying well, 155 yards from the flag and a safe 25 yards from that fairway bunker, which from now on can be ignored.

However, there are two bunkers guarding the elevated green and the flag is placed well back. Because the green is uphill, the ball must fly a little bit farther and higher.

1. The club you would usually choose for this distance is the no. 6 iron, but because the green is uphill, with menacing bunkers in the way, and the flag is deep in the green, with no trouble behind, you go for the no. 5 iron. Of course, if you feel that this shot is beyond your capabilities, play safe by placing the ball well short of the bunkers, leaving yourself the easiest shot you can.

2. Your pre-shot routine will take into account that you are going to have to play this ball slightly more forward in the stance and with your weight more on the right foot than usual. Your hands will then be just behind the ball. These changes in your set-up will, with a full, free swing, give you the increased height you need. As usual, the pre-shot routine will give the right feel for the shot to be played.

3. The ball is well on its way, and the finish of the swing finds you with your weight well forward, hands high, and the right foot pulled upright. This shot leaves you on the green with your chance of a birdie.

4. And here it is. Neither of your first two shots was necessarily perfect, but correct club choice for both the tee and the second shot has saved you a stroke. Using your mental capacity like this can save you many more.

DOWNHILL LIE

If there is one lie that most golfers find up-setting, it is when the ball must be played from a down-slope. The old inherent fear of not being able to get the ball in the air rears its ugly head once again, and panic takes over. This is needless, because with a little thought and a few changes in set-up and alignment, it will be possible for you to take your normal swing. As always, when confronted with a special shot, you should remember your mental training–relaxation, concentration, and target projection.

First of all, you need a club with more loft than the distance would normally require, as the ball will tend to fly lower and longer from this lie. Secondly, you want to strike the ball first and the grass after, which means the clubhead must follow the slope. This is made possible by standing

1. Pre-shot routine as usual. See the flight of the ball, starting to the left of target, due to the tendency of the ball to curve right at the end of its flight. Pick out the intermediate target. Take some practice swings until you feel that you have the correct swing for the shot required.

2. Address the ball, with your shoulder line parallel to the slope, but with more weight on the right foot.

3. (*Opposite*) Release your swing, arms flying freely from the body down the slope, finishing with good balance.

perpendicular to the slope, i.e. with your shoulders parallel to the incline. This position will prevent the club fastening in the grass on the backswing and will enable you to strike the ball before the ground on the downswing. Keeping your shoulders parallel to the incline, let your weight favour the right foot, to stop the body from moving past the ball before the club makes contact. If that should happen, the ball will fly way to the right. So: upper body down the slope, but weight more on the right foot, aim slightly to the left to offset the fade that occurs with this lie. Then take your normal swing.

UPHILL LIE

When faced with a ball that is lying on an uphill slope, the club you choose should be sufficient to offset the loss of distance through increased height that always happens from this lie. For instance, if the ball was lying on the level, you would use a no. 7 iron, but as the uphill lie will make it fly higher than normal, you choose a no. 5 iron and hold it slightly shorter (as if it were a no. 7 iron). Your shoulder line should be parallel to the slope and your weight should favour the left foot. This will assist correct timing and stop you keeping too much weight on the right foot, which would make the clubhead reach the ball too early, sending it way to the left. Aim slightly to the right of your target to offset the draw that occurs from an uphill lie. Then take your normal swing.

1. Take into consideration the uphill lie before choosing your club, which should be a slightly longer club than you would use if the ball was on the level. Stand behind the ball. Pick out your intermediate target, slightly to the right of the flag, and see in your imagination the successful flight of the ball.

2. Address the ball with the shoulder line parallel to the slope and with more weight on the left foot.

3. *(Opposite)* Use your normal swing. All necessary adjustments have already been made during set-up and alignment.

SIDEHILL LIE:
ball below your feet

This and the downhill lie already discussed are the two most problematic lies on the fairway. But again, a normal swing is possible here, if you make some changes to your set-up and alignment, and strive for good balance and posture, together with a steady head position. In order to ground the club correctly behind the ball on this side-slope lie, you must stand nearer the ball, or you won't hit it at its base. Take some practice swings to see where your clubhead makes contact with the ground. This will show you that the distance between the ball and your feet is less than in the normal lie.

You must also lean forward from the waist more than usual, but without losing your balance. In order to keep a correct posture throughout the swing, keep your weight back towards the heels and push out your behind. A normal swing from a severe slope will now do one of two things: the heel of the club will hit the ground first, or the upright swing, caused by this position, will send the ball way off to the right, so another adjustment is necessary. Aim to the left. This reduces the severity of the slope, creating better contact with the ball, and allows for the inevitable fade. All these changes made, go ahead and swing in the normal fashion.

1. Before taking your stance, stand behind the ball, visualize the ball flight, and pick out your intermediate target. Remember that the ball will curve to the right from this lie, so aim well left of the target.

2. A slightly shorter backswing to create a more aggressive strike, so that the ball will not fly too high or too far to the right.

The more upright swing caused by this lie tends to create more height, so you should take a club that is longer than you would first think necessary for the distance required.

SIDEHILL LIE:
ball above your feet

Another lie that requires special set-up and alignment, followed by a normal swing. With the sole of the club correctly grounded, the grip end of the shaft will be lower than normal. This causes a flatter swing. Therefore, stand more upright, with your weight well forward towards the soles of your feet, knees bent a little more than usual, and aim to the right to allow for the draw. These changes to your set-up and alignment made, take your normal swing. The flatter swing caused by this lie sends the ball lower, so take this into account when choosing your club.

1. Starting the backswing. The stance is to the right of the target, knees are bent more than usual, body is more upright .

2. The ball is well on its way to the right of the target, making a long, white blur on its way over the right-hand side of the bunker, before curving left to finish on the green.

THE LONG IRONS

These are the clubs that appear the least suitable for creating height and sending the ball any appreciable distance, as the long shaft and thin blade, with very little loft, in no way induce confidence. This causes the uncertain player to tighten first his hands and then his arms and shoulders. The results are all negative: the backswing becomes too fast and tends to shorten (otherwise he would "lose" the club on the backswing); clubhead speed is dissipated by excessive use of the shoulders, so he ends up "throwing" himself at the ball to make up for the lack of club-head speed.

If tempo was ever important in golf, it is when you are playing the long irons. Tempo is learned on the driving range, using the normal practice routine and swinging the club with exactly the same rhythm as the shorter clubs.

THE MENTAL APPROACH

You know from your shot-length profile how far you can expect the ball to fly with each club. Therefore, allow the club to do the work, with your normal, free swing.

Confidence gained in this manner will stand you in good stead in the future. And confidence breeds yet more confidence, leading invariably to success.

1. An important part of this pre-shot routine is to create extension by swinging the club backwards and forwards, allowing the arms to swing freely away from the body. This mini-swing, taken before striking the ball, is a way of reducing tension, which then allows you to swing the club in the correct, free arm movement particularly necessary when playing the long irons.

2. Pick out the intermediate target and place the clubhead behind the ball.

3. Go through your normal set-up and alignment routine. With your weight slightly to the right and your hands and shaft in a straight line, prepare to swing the club smoothly and freely back from the ball.

If you find that you have difficulty in playing your long irons on the golf course, imagine you are playing a lofted wood instead. The free swinging of the no. 3, 4, or 5 wood encourages the feeling of smoothness that you need in your long-iron play. Swinging the iron with the same amount of freedom and rhythm as if it were a lofted wood, encourages relaxation and gives you confidence in what you are about to do.

Until you have achieved stability with your long irons, you will find that a no. 5 or 7 wood is a sound investment.

It is inadvisable to take full practice swings before playing the long shots. It takes the muscles some time to return to their normal tension level after a full swing. Slow loosening-up half swings will help create correct path, feel, and tempo.

4. Swinging the arms freely and wide to a full backswing will promote the full shoulder turn necessary for good tempo when playing a long iron. Remember to complete your backswing before starting on the downswing.

5. The ball has been struck and the arms have passed through the hitting area. The weight has moved from right foot to left heel, while the weight of the clubhead brings the right side of the body into the shot, finishing in a full, free follow-through.

PLAYING FROM A DIVOT MARK

This often happens – what appears to be a perfect drive from the tee is ruined because some clever person has omitted to replace a divot, and your ball has come to rest just there. This will have a negative effect on your score only if you allow it to affect your composure. It is a challenge like any other, and this is what makes golf such a fascinating game. Don't see it as bad luck and become annoyed with whoever forgot to replace the divot, as this will be detrimental to clear thinking. Think instead in the present tense, of the situation at hand and how you will master it.

Always replace your divots. Even if you can play this shot well, perhaps your fellow golfers can't!

1. Can this be my ball after such a good drive?

2. Choose a club that is more lofted than the distance would suggest. Play the ball back in the stance, with the weight towards the left foot, aiming at your intermediate target, which here should be slightly right of the desired goal.

THE MENTAL APPROACH

The ability to manage this situation depends on how you can accept what has happened without getting annoyed. See the shot as an interesting challenge. Use your common sense and imagination as usual. Practise the shot, and you will find that it is not that difficult.

Having the hands in front of the ball and the weight towards the left foot will reduce the loft of the club, making the ball fly lower and roll longer than usual. The shortened backswing and solid arm movement, punching the ball out of this lie, will cause the ball to fly low, and, as with most well-struck low shots, it will curve left. Therefore, your intermediate target must be to the right, to offset this tendency. As usual, only intelligent practice on the practice ground will tell you how much to the right you need to aim.

3. Because you want to hit the ball with more punch than usual, the backswing should be shorter. Then with a strong left-arm movement, swing the club down and through, striking the ball first and the ground afterwards.

4. Finish the swing with the weight well forward on the left foot, hips turned to the left, shaft pointing at the target, and the toe of the club at the sky. This position ensures that the arms rather than the hands have been used, preventing a premature turning of the clubface to the left, or the striking of the ground before the ball.

WOOD SHOT WITH A DRAW

The ball is lying well on the fairway, 230 yards from the green. The bunker immediately in front should not be a problem, but it might frighten you into lifting your head a little too early to see the result of your shot. A steady head position will encourage a good strike and clear the bunker with no trouble at all. Therefore, forget about the bunker.

With a shot like this, aim is the most important factor. A draw (i.e., starting slightly to the right and curving back to the centre at the end) is your best bet here, because it enables you to create a little more distance. Because the clubface is slightly closed to create the draw, you are effectively turning the no. 4 wood into a no. 3, thereby sending the ball lower, with more roll, creating greater distance.

1. Because aim is so important, you must spend some extra time on planning the line of flight. Stand behind the ball and pick out the intermediate target, not in line with the flag but to its right.

2. Go through your usual set-up and alignment routine, making certain that your clubface is square to the intermediate target and your hands are turned slightly to the right, holding the shaft lightly.

THE MENTAL APPROACH

Your practice sessions have proved that the change of hand position and pressure will cause a draw. Therefore, you can with confidence aim to the right from this position, allow the swing to take its natural course, enjoying the feeling of being able to make the ball curve in the air at will. Another visit to the bank to make a deposit....

3. Clubface, stance, and body are now aligned to the right of the flag.

4. Because of the change of grip, the clubface has closed a little earlier, hitting the ball lower, and making it curve to the left towards the end of its flight. The ball passed low over the bunker to the right of the target, and then curved left, landing and rolling forward, before coming to rest on the green.

WOOD SHOT WITH A FADE

Here, the ball has landed on the right-hand side of the fairway, almost 300 yards from the green. After careful consideration of the lie and the target, you decide that a faded wood shot is necessary to give you a simple third shot onto the green. For a faded shot, you need a slightly open clubface, so increase the grip pressure and move the hands more to the left on the shaft. Because the ball will curve from left to right in the air, due to the open clubface, it will also fly a little quicker. So choose your target area with care, so as to ensure an easier third shot, preferably from a level lie and with no bunkers between it and the green.

Allow for this left-to-right curve when you aim, with everything aligned left of the target area: the intermediate target, the

1. Clubhead behind the ball, face square to the intermediate target, which is on a line to the left of the target area.

2. Starting the club on the downswing, with a strong left arm pulling it down towards the ball.

clubhead, your feet, and the rest of your body. Even from a mediocre lie, the no. 3 wood, with a slightly open face, is the one to use, as the more lofted woods tend to reduce the fade spin. (This is something worth remembering for occasions when you have out-of-bounds markers bordering the right-hand side of the fairway.)

3. Just after impact, the left hip is clearing the way to allow the left arm to continue through.

4. The finish position, with the hips and shoulders turned slightly more to the left and a little flatter than usual, is produced by the strong left-arm movement through the ball. The ball started towards the left, curved right, and finished in the target area.

THE LONG RUNNING SHOT

The long running shot is especially useful when it is difficult to see where the green begins and how deep in the green the flag is placed. It can also be used when the ground is hard and there is a slight ridge or bank in front of the green. The ball will travel low, bouncing in front of the green, hopping further forward up the ridge and rolling onto the putting surface.

This is a good shot to play if the ball is lying badly and it is difficult to judge how far it will fly through the air before landing.

1. This is the follow-through position after a practice swing designed to send the ball 70 yards. The weight is on the left foot, and the upper body is stationary. Relaxed arm movement. Hands softened.

2. Address position. Intermediate target taken, weight favouring the left foot, ball centred in stance, hands over the ball. The choice is a no. 6 iron. Check the imaginary flight, bounce, and roll.

3. *(Opposite)* The ball has been struck with hands and weight well forward, club closing to create minimal backspin, sending the ball low, some 50 yards, to bounce up the ridge and roll towards the target.

THE MENTAL APPROACH

Target projection is, as usual, important here, together with the correct feeling and knowledge that the ball will bounce and roll freely, due to the choice of club and the relaxed movement through the ball.

Playing from sand can be made easier than you
think, if you use your mental training.

CHAPTER 7

PLAYING FROM SAND

The sand iron, or bunker club, differs from the rest of the irons inasmuch as its trailing edge (or bounce) is nearer the ground than its leading edge when the shaft is held upright and the clubface is square. The effect of the sand-iron shot is that sand is displaced and compressed behind the ball, so that sand and ball are splashed into the air. The object of the sand iron's trailing edge is to prevent the club from digging into the sand and stopping. The more you open the club, the lower the trailing edge becomes, and the less chance there is of fastening in the sand.

The better the lie, the more you open the clubface. The deeper the ball lies in the sand, the more the clubface should be closed, causing the leading edge to penetrate deeper into the sand under the ball. Although the clubhead in the latter case fastens in the sand, the displaced sand has sufficient power to propel the ball into the air.

Sand – problem or not?

We have all heard that the bunker shots are the easiest shots in the game, because this is the only time you don't need to hit the ball. Whatever truth there might be in this ancient golf saying, many golfers believe that ending up in a sand bunker is one of the worst things that can happen to them. This is the nightmare situation which causes their game to go to pieces. They see themselves flailing away in the bunker, moving as much sand as an excavator but not moving the ball more than a foot or two, and even then deeper into the sand. This need not be the case, as playing well from the bunker is no great problem, if you understand why the club is constructed as it is and what happens during the swing. This knowledge, together with positive experiences of bunker shots, will build up your confidence, so that next time, a ball in the sand will not mean the end of the world.

The clubface

Most good golfers open the club the same amount to the right of the flag as they stand to the left of the target line. The set-up and alignment for the sand shot from a good lie are an open stance, the ball in line with the left foot, the hands over or slightly in front of the ball, and the club slightly open. *Very important!* Open the clubface before you take your grip. Otherwise, the clubface will return to its original position at impact.

When addressing the ball with the open clubface, be careful not to have the heel of the club too near the ball, as it is then easy to hit the ball at the junction of the shaft and the blade. This is avoided by taking your address position with ball towards the toe of the club.

The swing

The swing for the normal bunker shot is a free, easy arm movement, pulling the club down to the ball, striking the sand which, with its weight, lifts the ball out of the bunker and onto the putting surface. As previously mentioned, if the ball is lying well, then the club must be opened, lowering the trailing edge to prevent the club from going too deeply into the sand. Should the ball be slightly deeper in the sand, then the clubface need not be open so much.

If the ball is buried in the sand, then the clubface must be closed so that its leading edge digs into the sand, expelling the ball. This swing is different from that for a good lie (the smooth, full, free arm swing): the wrists must break more abruptly on the backswing and the angle of approach is much steeper, causing the leading edge to dig into the sand just behind the ball.

Because you cannot ground your club in a hazard, the only way to feel the texture of the sand is with your feet, when you walk into the bunker and take your stance.

LIE	STANCE	SWING
Good	Ball in line with left instep, club open, feet, hips, and shoulder point to left as much as the club is open to the right; weight centred.	Free, easy swing with an early wrist break. Full follow-through. Light grip.
Half-buried	Ball in line with left heel, club and feet square to target. Weight favours left foot.	Free swing with wrists broken earlier than before. Firmer grip.
Buried	Ball back of centre, club closed, feet, hips, and shoulders point to right as much as club is closed to the left. Weight on left foot.	Firm, resolute grip, wrists break early, sharp down-swing with right hand pushing into sand. No follow-through.

A correctly executed sand shot, played from a
good lie in a greenside bunker with a high lip.

GREENSIDE BUNKER:
from a good lie

The ball is lying well in the bunker, about 10 feet from the lip, which is only 3 feet high. Target projection has to take place without the benefit of real practice swings, as the rules forbid you to ground your club in the bunker. Therefore, take some practice swings outside the bunker, to get the feel for the swing needed.

The sand is dry but quite compact. Plenty of arm swing will enable you to play this shot in a leisurely, tension-free fashion, which is important when playing this type of shot from greenside bunkers.

1. Align your feet and body to the left of the flag and hold your club so that the clubface is open (pointing to the right of the flag). The open clubface will ensure that the trailing edge, or bounce, of the club will strike the sand first. With your weight centred and the ball just inside the left heel, and your hands in front of the ball, hold the club lightly and a little further down on the shaft. Address the ball towards the toe of the club, with clubhead above the sand and behind the ball.

Visualize the stroke that you are going to play – the clubhead splashing through the sand, the ball lifting over the lip of the bunker, landing on the green, and rolling to the flag.

2. Break the wrists early to create a steep backswing. On the downswing, make sure that the left arm and left side lead the club towards the sand.

THE MENTAL APPROACH

Anger with yourself at getting in there and anxiety about how to get out will cause you to tighten up and be unable to swing properly. Holding the club too tightly causes a loss of tempo (a shortening and quickening of the back swing), which produces yet another fault, a vicious throw of the club towards the ball. All you have left is the hope that blind strength instead of common sense, awareness, and confidence will do the job. It won't. Your mental bank manager will turn down your request for a loan here.

If you find this situation to be nerve-wracking and to be the cause of your losing strokes, practise it as often as you can. Learn to be friends with the sand, and also learn how high and how far the ball will fly when you have the clubface open different amounts. Awareness and practice will give you confidence.

3. Swing through the ball, the trailing edge splashing into and through the sand, and continue to a high, unhurried finish.

GREENSIDE BUNKER:
from a buried lie

There is no reason for panic when faced with a buried lie like this. The important thing to remember is that it is the club, not you, that will do the job. With the ball lying deep, there is no point in opening the clubface, as the club would simply bounce over the ball, catching it towards its top. When playing these shots, close the clubface before gripping the club slightly firmer than usual, to prevent the sand stopping the club too early. The fact that the downswing is sharp means that there won't be too much sand between the clubface and the ball, so it will fly out lower and faster, and roll more than usual; therefore you need less backswing and clubhead speed than you would imagine.

1. Here, we see the position of the ball, close to the right foot, the closed clubface, and the toe of the club pointing at the ball, with the hands marginally in front.

2. The hands break sharply on the backswing, and there is very little body movement. At the top of the backswing, the hands are at chest height.

3. On the downswing, the right hand pushes the blade of the club deeply into the ground to strike the sand as near as possible behind the ball.

4. Just after impact, the right hand has pushed the club into and through the sand.

5. *(Opposite)* The follow-through ends with the clubhead still closed and the ball leaving the sand low and just to the right of the flag, rolling much faster than you would have expected. Note the body alignment.

GREENSIDE BUNKER:
the high shot from soft sand

When you play from soft sand, you must have enough arm movement to offset the cushioning effect of the sand, which can stop the club abruptly, preventing it from flying the ball high and softly onto the green, so there is no reason to shorten the backswing and increase the tempo. In fact, the opposite is the correct move: lengthen the swing and slow down the tempo. The lengthened swing will continue through the sand. The slower tempo will give you the correct depth of sand and will not send the ball too far. Do not try to help the ball up – let the club and the swing do it.

Take your practice swings outside the bunker. Concentrate on achieving a rhythm and a movement that will enable you to *see* the successful flight and finish of the ball.

1. Your weight favours the right foot, the clubface is well open and pointing to the right of the target, and body alignment is to the left to create a slight out-to-in swing in relation to the flag. Hold the club with a light grip and your hands over the ball.

2. On the backswing, your arms should be shoulder high, with a great deal of wrist movement.

3. The downswing is to be unhurried, with the left arm and hip pulling the club down to strike the sand the correct distance behind the ball.

4. The swing continues all the way through to a high finish, and the compressed sand lifts the ball over the lip, to drop softly onto the green.

THE MENTAL APPROACH

Awareness of the effect of the texture of the sand is important when playing from this kind of lie. The full, free leisurely swing creates a stroke which from grass would have sent the ball twice as far.

GREENSIDE BUNKER:
the short shot from hard-packed sand

The ball is lying on hard-packed sand, with only a low lip between it and the hole, which is 20 feet in from the edge of the green. The club used can be either the pitching wedge or the sand iron. The firm sand will not affect the club other than to cause it to bounce – so much that the ball may be topped, so you need to make some change in your set-up and alignment.

The ball should be centred between the feet and your weight equally divided. With your stance square to the flag, hold the club firmly in both hands but with slightly more pressure in the fingers of the left, and the hands directly above the ball.

1. The backswing is completed – the arms are chest high and the wrists fully broken.

2. The downswing is created by pulling the club down to the ball with the left arm, the right hand flipping under the stretched left arm.

The right knee follows the swing to the position shown here, the left hand and the arm stopping the club before it is parallel with the ground. This gives the ball considerable backspin, making it stop very quickly after landing, so that it does not run too far past the flag.

3. Do not forget to rake the sand after you have played your shot!

THE FAIRWAY BUNKER SHOT

Not all bunkers are placed around the green. Fairway bunkers, a considerable distance from the flag, require a different technique and a different mental attitude. Your first reaction is to want to hit the ball as far as you can out of the bunker, as you still have quite a way to go to the green. But sometimes, the lie of the ball can mean that you have no alternative except to play the ball out with your sand iron, perhaps not even in the direction of the green.

As usual, routine is very important, and imagination and confidence are necessary.

Club choice

Probably the most important thing when playing a long bunker shot from a distance of, say, 140 yards from the flag, is the fact that you must choose a club that will easily clear the front lip of the bunker and will create the distance required. If the ball is lying well, you choose a club with the intention of striking the ball first and the sand afterwards. Having such a distance to cover, hitting the sand first would reduce the effect of the swing, and you will find the ball well short.

Set-up and alignment

Your chances of hitting the ball first are best if the ball is slightly back in the stance and your hands are slightly forward of the ball, with your weight more on the left foot. The club chosen should have enough loft – remember that having your hands in front of the ball reduces the loft – to give sufficient height to the ball to clear the lip of the bunker. Too often, a well-struck bunker shot flies too low, hits the front lip of the bunker, and rolls back down, just because the club chosen had too little loft.

As in all bunker shots (including those from a greenside bunker), make sure your feet are firmly embedded in the sand. And when you play a long shot from a fairway bunker, your right foot should be at an angle to the target line, so that there is no likelihood that you move your right foot on the backswing, thus ruining your shot.

A 90-yard sand shot.

FAIRWAY BUNKER:
playing an iron shot

The ball is lying well and the bunker is not deep, so you do not need too lofted a club to clear the front lip. However, remembering that you will de-loft the club by having your hands in front of the ball, you take a club with more loft than you would have considered necessary. If, for instance, you believe that you need a no. 6 iron to carry the lip of the bunker and to move the ball the distance required, you choose a no. 7 iron, because, when you put your hands in front of the ball, you de-loft the club to a no. 6.

Having more weight on the left foot and your hands in front of the ball will cause the ball to curve slightly from left to right in the air. Take this into consideration when aligning yourself with the target. Set yourself up a little to the left of the target so as to allow the ball to curve from left to right, remembering that it will stop fairly quickly after landing.

THE MENTAL APPROACH

Not enough bunker practice – especially from the fairway bunkers – means that you have not enough experience upon which to build your awareness and confidence. You need to have those regular positive experiences of playing from sand, deposited in your mental bank account.

In a bunker, it is important that you get your priorities right. The first priority is to get the ball out of the bunker. The second is to make your next shot easier. The third is to achieve the correct direction and distance.

1. Practice swings must be taken outside the bunker, of course. Take them in line with the target, having examined the lie and chosen your club. Create a feeling of confidence by visualizing the successful result of the practice swing, which must give you the correct feel for the swing needed.

2. In the bunker. The lie being good, the clubface should be slightly open. Move your weight more to your left foot and place your hands in front of the ball. This stance has the further advantage of producing a slightly steeper backswing, which increases the chances of hitting the ball *first* and the sand after, a must in the long bunker shot.

3. The same picture as **2**, taken from the side to show the position of the ball – back in the stance and behind the hands.

4. Just after impact. The ball has been struck first, the sand afterwards. The weight is almost fully on the left foot.

5. Continuing to the full follow-through position, with arms flowing freely, pulling the body to the normal finish position.

FAIRWAY BUNKER:
playing the wood shot

There is no reason why you should not take a wood to play a long shot from a fairway bunker, if the ball is lying well and the bunker is shallow.

Because the longer clubs produce less backspin than the shorter clubs, any side-spin produced tends to be greater than expected, so when playing a wooden club from a bunker and having the face open, the ball is likely to curve in the air a great deal.

Aim therefore well to the left of the desired target.

The swing movement is similar to the normal full swing you would use on the fairway. Good balance, and above all a smooth tempo, are necessary to achieve a good strike.

THE MENTAL APPROACH

The normal reaction when you find your tee shot in a fairway bunker is annoyance and fear. Common sense and confidence in your ability to play the most suitable shot can prevent you losing a stroke in this situation. Don't always try for maximum length, but pick a realistic target that you know is within your shot-length capability. The condition of the sand, the lie of the ball, and the height of the bunker's lip will tell you what club and shot to play.

1. The ball is lying well in the middle of the bunker, which is quite shallow. The sand is firm. Pick out your target area and choose your club. Here, the no. 3 wood is the choice.

2. Set-up and alignment. Ball slightly further back in stance than for a normal fairway wood, and everything aimed to the left. Clubface open so as to bounce the sole of the club into the sand, preventing the front edge from digging in and stopping abruptly.

3. The ball is struck and well on its way, starting left and then curving back onto the fairway. The arms are freely swinging to a full, finish position.

A golfing challenge is met – the ball is well on its
way out of the rough.

CHAPTER EIGHT

IT'S NOT TOUGH IN THE ROUGH

Ending up in the rough is a normal golfing occurrence. Expect it, and learn to handle it as a natural part of the game. Many golfers get so upset when they land in the rough that their game goes to pieces. Your mental approach is all-important here, and you must bring into play all the mental strength that you have taught yourself in your mental training sessions.

No regrets!
First and foremost, accept the fact that you are in the rough and don't go into paroxysms of rage and self-accusation. Then start searching, and, having found the ball, identify it as yours. After this, turn all your concentration to the actual shot that you are going to have to play.

Examine the lie
Is the ball playable? If not, play by the rule book and drop away with a one-shot penalty, or go back and play the shot again, with loss of stroke and distance. Remember that you can make matters much worse by trying the impossible. Your impossible

shot can put you deeper into trouble, with even more strokes to be added to your score, as you hack your way out, yard by yard.

If the ball is playable, then see what your alternatives are. The shortest way onto the fairway may mean hitting the ball away from the hole but could also mean that your next shot will be simpler, giving you the opportunity to save a stroke.

The bad lie
If the ball is deep in the grass, the only way to get it out well is to strike it with as little grass as possible between it and the clubhead. You do this by shifting your weight more to your left, opening the clubface, breaking your wrists earlier than usual, and letting your hands lead at impact. This means that the downswing is sharper, causing the ball to pop up out of the deep lie and out onto the fairway. Because the ball is lying deep, the grass in front may well stop your follow-through, so be prepared that the ball may not fly very far and choose your target area accordingly.

PLAYING UP AND OUT OF THE ROUGH

A slice from the tee has landed the ball in the rough, where bushes block your way out onto the fairway again. This is a typical nightmare situation, in which you must keep cool and bring your common sense and imagination into action. Don't rush up to the ball, but approach it calmly, examine the situation, and let your common sense tell you which club to pick to get that ball to fly high, over the bushes, and out onto the fairway.

1. You find that the ball is lying quite well, so it should be possible to fly it over the bushes in the direction of the flag. Visualize the necessary trajectory of the ball, and this will tell you what club you need. Here, a no. 8 iron is the best choice to give you the right height.

2. Your practice swings must create the right feeling for the swing you need. If the first practice swing is not convincing, i.e., does not make you feel that the imagined shot will have the correct trajectory, take some more swings, until you are sure that you have found the optimal swing for this shot.

THE MENTAL APPROACH

If you find that you are not able to treat this situation calmly, use the relaxing exercises to help you loosen up and concentrate.

Your imagination will help you to visualize the flight of the ball during your practice swings. Remember that you can take as many practice swings as necessary, until you feel that you have the right swing feeling to get the ball up and away.

3. At the finish of the correct practice swing, you can follow the imaginary flight of the ball, seeing the perfect result of your shot.

4. Now put the club behind the ball, and let your swing flow automatically, keeping your head still until well after the ball has been struck.
In the picture, you can see the ball as it flies through the air, over the bush and out onto the fairway. Back into business!

FROM THE ROUGH TO THE FAIRWAY

Here, you are confronted by two problems: **1)** you must play from deep rough and **2)** you must aim so that you don't hit one of the trees and end up in the rough once again.

As usual when you end up in the rough, first you have to find and identify your ball. Then decide whether it is playable. Next comes choice of shot to be played and subsequent selection of club. In this situation, with the ball lying deep in the grass, the sand wedge is your best bet.

THE MENTAL APPROACH

Your mental reaction to this type of double problem can often be a kind of "freezing", so that you don't think through the situation properly. "Unfreeze" by some deep breathing and relaxation exercises, as you are considering the situation. Then concentrate on the practice swings and the visualization of a successful shot from there.

1. Pick out the correct line to the right of the big tree, taking into account also the sand on the other side of the fairway and the decided target area for your shot. Pick out an intermediate target that will give you the desired line.

2. After practice swings that give you the right feel for the shot, go through your set-up and alignment routine as usual, but with extra care so that your swing path is sure to send the ball to the right of the big tree.

3. Break your wrists early, swinging more upright to prevent the club catching in the long grass and also to give you a steeper downswing for better contact.

4. *(Opposite)* At impact, your hands are ahead of the ball and – due to the steep angle of descent – the clubface will make contact with the ball with as little grass as possible in between, sending the ball high and onto the fairway.

THE SHOT IN BETWEEN

Here we have a situation in which the ball is not lying well and has to fly low and straight because of the trees. Matters are further complicated by the two bunkers and the position of the flag. The question here is, "Can I play this shot near the flag?"

Common sense says no. Discretion is the better part of valour, so the shot to choose will be to the left of the big bunker, finishing on or near the green, leaving a long putt or a simple chip.

THE MENTAL APPROACH

Common sense will tell you the shot that you are able to play with the greatest chance of success. It will answer such questions as, "Which club am I safe with in a lie like this?" and "Will the ball be low enough to bounce and roll on the foregreen before reaching the green?" Your common sense is built upon previous situations of this kind that you have come across, either in play or in practice. Here, because of the lie and the distance the ball should roll, a medium iron is the choice.

Having chosen the shot and the club, your imagination will be triggered off by your practice swings, enabling you to visualize the successful shot, low enough to avoid the branches and aimed well enough to fly straight between the trees. This target projection will give you the confidence to play the shot as imagined. Do not change your mind, but play the shot as you "saw" it, letting the swing happen of its own accord. Remember that the actual swing should be a copy of your successful practice swings, with exactly the same tempo.

1. Identify the ball and examine the lie. Consider your alternatives. Having made your decision, choose the intermediate target, giving yourself plenty of room to the left of the bunker. Visualize the successful flight, bounce, and roll of the ball until it stops.

2. Having taken enough practice swings to create the right length of backswing necessary to send the ball the required distance, place the clubhead carefully behind the ball. Address the ball, with the hands slightly in front of the ball and your weight towards the left foot.

3. See in your mind's eye the successful shot just before you allow the swing to take place, repeating your practice swing exactly.

4. *(Opposite)* The shot has been taken and the ball is on its way. The clubhead is well through and low to the ground. The head is still and the upper body has not moved forward, although the weight is even more towards the left foot.

A LOW DRAW AROUND THE TREES

The draw is the shot to choose when you want to hit the ball with a slight curve to the left at the end of its flight, to avoid an obstruction in your path. Before attempting a shot like this during a game, you must have practised it, bearing in mind the ball-flight laws discussed on pages 15–20. The ball will start on the line upon which you swing the club and finish by curving in the direction of the clubface at impact.

Ensure that the swing path is to the right of the trees, thus starting the ball to the right. The clubface must be pointing at the target to get the ball to curve left after it passes the trees. In other words, the clubface will be closed to the swing path but square to the target. Remember that the ball will roll considerably further than usual, due to the fact that the club is de-lofted.

1. Here, a pull has caused the ball to finish in the left-hand rough, leaving no possibility of a straight shot because of trees directly in line with the target. So, a draw is the only solution.

THE MENTAL APPROACH

Any shot with intentional curve must have been visualized most vividly before you attempt it. A diffuse picture of the ball flight in your mind will almost certainly result in failure to accomplish your objective.

If you are over-anxious about a shot like this, you will find it more difficult to visualize a successful conclusion. If you are having trouble in imprinting a positive picture in your mind's eye, move away and start your pre-shot routine from the very beginning.

N.B. When curving a ball around an obstacle, remember to give yourself a good safety margin so that the ball is sure to clear the obstruction by a comfortable distance. So many shots actually hit the obstacle they are supposed to avoid, because they are not started sufficiently to the left or right.

Also worth remembering is the fact that a ball curving to the left will roll more, while a ball curving to the right will roll less than a normal shot.

2. Remove all loose impediments around the ball to give you the best chance of a good strike.

3. Having taken a number of practice swings to achieve the right feel for the shot, you address the ball. It should be back in the stance, so that your hands are in front of the ball. Your grip should be lighter and your hands placed more to the right on the shaft than usual.

4. A short backswing, with the club low to the ground, and with very little wrist movement is what is required here.

5. The right hand is passing the left, making the clubface point to the left of the swing path. This in turn will cause the ball to curve to the left after passing the trees.

6. The follow-through. Your arms have rotated completely, closing the clubface.

TARGET PROJECTION FROM THE ROUGH

The ball is lying reasonably well in semi-rough, 120 yards from the flag. There is a bunker to the left but there is plenty of room on the green to the right of the flag. The shot to play from this position should land the ball just in front of the green, so that it bounces once or twice before rolling slowly onto the putting surface. Clear target projection is necessary to achieve the correct carry. Remember that shots from thick grass lack backspin, so that the ball will bounce and roll forward.

1. Take a good look at the lie of the ball and the distance to the flag. Very little backspin is possible from this lie, so the choice of club is important, as the ball will bounce and roll forward after landing. Choose an intermediate target.

2. A no. 8 iron being the best choice, take your practice swings to build up the correct feeling for the amount of movement required.

3. *(Opposite)* Address the ball, with the clubface square to the intermediate target. Visualize the shot as planned, seeing the ball bounce just short and roll onto the green.

LOW CHIP BACK ONTO THE FAIRWAY

The ball is lying quite well in semi-rough but normal flight is impossible as over-hanging branches are in the way. A low chip shot is necessary to get the ball out from under the trees, putting you in a good posi-tion for your next shot. This situation nor-mally causes people to swing down faster than necessary, so before your practice swings, you should loosen up your arms by swinging the club smoothly to and fro.

A no. 5 iron, held low on the shaft, with hands in front of the ball, will prevent the ball from flying too high.

1. Examine the lie of the ball and be extra careful to choose the best line under the trees. Loosen up your arms by swinging the club gently to and fro.

2. Take your practice swings to create the right length and speed necessary. This shot demands a little more wrist action on the backswing, thus increasing the speed of the downswing without rushing it.

THE MENTAL APPROACH

As always when playing special shots like this, anxiety is likely to creep in and cause you to look up too early. Good target projection will give you the confidence to prevent this and enable you to remain quite still until well after the ball has left the club.

Common sense will tell you what you can expect to achieve from this lie. With the longer club and the hands in front of the ball, it will fly low, come out rather quickly, and therefore bounce and roll a little more than usual.

3. Intermediate target selection and set-up routine. Hands low on the shaft and in front, with the ball back in the stance, will keep the ball low.

4. The finish of the low chip shot leaves the clubhead low to the ground and the hands firm on the shaft to ensure straight flight.

THROUGH THE TREES FROM A SIDEHILL LIE

The ball is lying well but on a sidehill. Because it is above the level of your feet, your swing will be flatter and the ball will tend to curve to the left. Also complicating the situation is the fact that you want to keep the ball under the branches, so you must have reduced body movement, which also tends to make the ball curve left in the air. Therefore, you must start it more towards the right-hand tree than towards the target. The presence of the two bunkers should not affect your mental approach here, because they don't come into play.

1. Take a good look at the lie of the ball and pick out your intermediate target with care. In this situation, you must start the ball on the correct target line, which is to the right of the flag, as you know that the ball will curve left.

2. After some practice swings to create the right feeling of length, place the clubhead carefully behind the ball, and aim at your intermediate target, which is to the right of the flag. Thereafter, go through your set-up and alignment routine.

THE MENTAL APPROACH

With the number of difficulties confronting you in this situation, it is of paramount importance to have a relaxed body and a quiet mind. Knowledge, common sense, imagination, and confidence are your allies: knowledge that the ball is likely to curve to the left from this position; common sense to tell you which club to choose and to shorten your backswing to prevent the ball flying too high; and imagination to create clear target projection. Thereafter, you will have the confidence to allow the swing to happen.

3. Holding the club a little lower than usual on the shaft to offset the fact that the ball is above your feet, swing the club back hip-high, keeping the clubhead low to the ground.

4. The follow-through. The ball is well on its way and to the right of the flag, as planned. The swinging of the arms is sufficient to send the ball the required distance, so the body remains fairly passive.

How did it go? Enjoyable hours on the golf
course in the company of good people are
rounded off with a check through the scorecard.

CHAPTER 9

PLAYING, COMPETING, WINNING

Golf is a highly competitive game in which you are your only opponent, whether you play in a fourball or on your own. Competing stroke-for-stroke with somebody can lead you into a hopeless situation from which recovery is impossible. For instance, if you play with someone much better than you and you try to match him stroke for stroke, then your inevitable failure will upset your game and make you play far below your capability. Likewise, if you play against someone with a much higher handicap than you, your own score would be far below normal if you were satisfied with beating him by, say, one or two strokes. Instead of competing with others, compete with yourself. Compare your score with your handicap and with your game on the actual day you are playing. Then you will be able to concentrate on your game, not allowing yourself to be upset if something goes wrong.

Golf is not nice, it's human!
When you play a round of golf, either in a friendly game or in a competition, you are not only taking part in the game, you are also a spectator. You see all the time how well or how badly the other players are doing, and this can affect your own game. Say that you are going out as second man on the first tee. The first player out tees up his ball and hits it a beautiful drive straight down the fairway, a good 200 yards. And you have to follow that performance! Your physical prowess has been challenged in a very macho-like way. So either you get up there and swing your club like a true caveman challenged about his virility, and you smash the ball way out of bounds, or you are intimidated by this performance and become afraid of making a fool of yourself. Your nerves fail you, and you mis-hit, thus confirming your poor opinion of yourself.

The opposite is also true. If the first player out duffs the ball, it is far easier for you to stride confidently up to your ball and hit a fine drive. Why? Because there is less pressure on, now that someone else has made a bit of a show of himself, and if you do the same thing, then you have a comrade in misfortune. Another reason could be that you are quite sure that you couldn't possibly make such an ass of yourself as the first player, and so, you are relaxed and confident. Not "nice" perhaps, but very human.

Don't compare!

Don't become involved in your fellow player's game or score, and *never* compare them during the game. It will only lead you into all kinds of mental conflicts (annoyance or shame that you are wishing somebody ill – or at least his game – jealousy, and so on). Stay detached and, if he is playing very well, say to yourself, "Jack is playing fantastically today. I hope he'll lower his handicap. Maybe he'll even get a prize!" Then concentrate on your own game and remember that your chances of winning depend on how well *you* play, not on how badly Jack plays. Admittedly, this is easier said than done, but positive self-talk like this will help you to be detached about others and to remember that you are playing against yourself – with *your* handicap and *your* game on the day – and *not* your fellow players.

CHECKLIST FOR PLAYING, COMPETING, WINNING

1. Think only in the present tense.
Don't dwell on any bad shots that you make and don't think about the second next hole which always gives you problems.

2. Switch on and off your concentration.
Always keep changing your concentration gear. Let your mind idle in between shots. Admire the scenery. Enjoy the company of your fellow players. Then get into top gear and concentrate fully on the stroke you are about to play.

3. Use positive self-talk.
Speak positively to yourself all the time. Your internal dialogue should always be encouraging: "Well done! What a chip!" Keep the positive thoughts flowing.

Never berate yourself for a bad shot. Accept it and then look forward to how well you are going to play the next shot.

4. Accept the challenge of the ball where it lies.
A challenge will increase your flow of adrenalin, and heighten your perception and competitive urge. So don't groan and give up everything for lost when you find your ball in a divot on the fairway. Rise to the challenge! You know you can!

5. Keep up the right rhythm.
Playing at a good steady rhythm will help you to take the time necessary to prepare for each stroke, so that you are not going to get into a breathless way of playing.

6. Losing is not the end of the world.
So what happens if you don't win? Is the world going to end? Remember to have a little distance to this wonderful game that we all love. It *is* a wonderful game if you allow yourself to enjoy it.

The challenge of the course

Each time you play, you are taking up the challenge of the course, testing your ability against it, and enjoying your battle with it, one shot at a time. Don't count scores before you have finished play, even after nine holes, and never compare your score for a hole with a previous score. Don't think about past or future scores, but play each hole as it comes, and never forget why you play golf – for enjoyment!

Preparing to play

Pre-game preparations are an important part of playing. You set the tone for the day's golf before you step out to the first tee, in fact even before you leave home. Check your golf bag and other gear in good time before you leave, so that you don't have to rush around in a panic looking for some missing piece of equipment. This means, too, that you won't have the upsetting experience of discovering that something is missing when you get out to the club.

Before you start to play, you make a plan for your round. You have, of course, played the round mentally a couple of times during the last few days, visualizing yourself playing each hole within the bounds of your capability (no holes in one, no impossible drives!). Your plan for the round should be dominated by only one thought for the day, not by several. For instance, your thought for the day might be, "Complete the backswing *before* starting the downswing!" If you have several thoughts for the day, your concentration will be split between them.

Once at the club, you are looking forward to the game with great anticipation. Get into a good golfing mood by checking your golf clubs, lifting them out of the bag, looking at them, feeling them. Make sure that

Part of your pre-match routine is to check that you have all your clubs properly positioned in the bag and that you have everything necessary to get around those eighteen holes.

each club is correctly placed in the bag. Check your other gear, too – scorecard and pencil, rule book, change of glove. Go into the clubhouse and check the local rules. Then spend some time relaxing and chatting to your friends. Remember that golf is a pastime to be enjoyed in the company of friendly people, so make your contribution to a friendly atmosphere at your club by being cheerful and open.

Then go out on the practice ground and warm up (see pages 35–37). Play perhaps twenty shots, observing the flight of the ball carefully to establish how your swing is working on that particular day. If your

155

Always make a round plan – even if you know the course well. Your swing on that particular day or the current weather may require an adjustment to your ordinary plan for that course.

practice shots show a tendency to fade, then your shot for the day is a fade – always play the shot that you are sure that you can repeat. This will help you to make a round plan. Take ten minutes to think through the course today and how you intend to play it, given the present state of your game.

Making a round plan is simply thinking through each hole, consulting the course map on the score card to refresh your memory. As you should have done this several times in the previous days when mentally preparing yourself for the competition, this will be quite easy. Imagine successful shots at those holes that seem always to give you problems. Consider how you will play them, taking care to give yourself lots of margin so that you avoid the various hazards. Remember that you should always choose the lesser of two evils when planning a stroke. If you must choose between a target area near a deep sand bunker on the left or near a shallow one on the right, choose the area near the shallow bunker. Or if your shot might land in water or out-of-bounds, then choose the shot that, if hit badly, would cost you less.

Planning like this is helpful to keep your feet firmly on the ground, whether things are going brilliantly or badly. It will also help you to play each shot for what it is – the three-foot putt is as important as the 200-yard drive. Furthermore, a proper plan will help you avoid trying for unrealistic goals, for instance, expecting to reach all par-4 greens with the second shot.

Then, properly warmed up and with a definite plan for the round in your mind, you go out to the first tee in the best possible mood to play well.

Always carry out the same pre-game routine. Remember how important the feeling of *deja vu* is for your mental well-being. If you can conjure up that pleasant feeling of having done it all before *and enjoyed it*, you are going to feel at home in the clubhouse and on the course. Going through the same pre-game routine each time will prod you to recall that enjoyable atmosphere which is one of the keys to successful playing.

At the first tee

Get to the first tee a little before you are due to start. Put the waiting time to good use, first of all with your deep-breathing exercises to relax hands, arms, legs, and torso (in that order). This will assist you to relax mentally.

Now check the position of the tee. Is it further forward or back than usual? What effect will this have on where your ball will land? Is the wind blowing so strongly that it will affect ball flight? Pick out two balls of the same make but with different numbers. Note them. The second one is if you have to play a provisional ball during the round. If you are beginning to feel tense, continue with your deep breathing, or use the clench-and-release method to relax again.

When the players in front of you have left the tee, take a couple of practice swings to reproduce the swing you had on the practice ground and to establish a good rhythm and tempo, seeing in your mind's eye a successful result of each practice swing. Then choose the place for your peg carefully, tee up the ball, and play your first shot, using a smooth and unhurried swing, an exact copy of your successful practice swing.

Between shots

Your ability to relax and turn off your concentration between shots is going to have a great effect on your result. Once you have played your shot from the tee, you move swiftly off the tee to allow the next player in the ball to play his stroke. Then you all walk off down the fairway. During the time it takes to reach the first ball, you can do three things: relax and enjoy the scenery, breathing deeply and thinking of nothing; relax and chat with your fellow players about anything except the shot played or

Pick out two balls: one to play with and one in case you need to play a provisional shot. Note make and number.

the shot to come; or worry yourself to death with self-accusations about the shot that you just played or with anxiety about the shot to come. Which of these three things do you usually do? Which of these three things do you enjoy least?

So relax and walk lightly down the fairway, head high and arms swinging in a relaxed way. Think only in the present tense. It's good to be out on a golf course, far away from the worries and troubles of everyday life, doing one of the things you enjoy most in life. If you see anyone slouching along with his head hanging, you can be sure that they are not enjoying their game. Their scores are going to show it, too.

Keep a constant pace throughout the game, even between holes. If you have had a birdie on the seventh hole, don't rush to the eighth tee with the intention of getting off a good drive for another birdie. Wait until your fellow players have holed their putts and then move off to the next tee at a steady pace. Don't rush anything in golf. Get into the right rhythm! A relaxed body, a quiet mind, and a confident attitude will help your play to be consistent and enjoyable.

If you watch top-class players playing in a tournament, notice how most of them behave between shots, keeping a steady pace as they walk along, not looking around and allowing outer circumstances to affect their few moments of relaxation before they must again switch on their powers of concentration to the full, for the next shot.

Winning

In any game, there will be just one winner. His golf may be only adequate, but his ability to perform well when it is necessary is the strongest weapon in his arsenal.

Winners have an aura of assuredness, are confident in their own prowess, and have complete control of their emotions.

In order to be a winner, it is necessary to understand and even experience defeat. Everybody plays badly on occasion, but only some people know how to learn from the experience. If you find that you are playing badly, don't dwell on it, but learn from it.

Remember, the winner always plays in the present tense.

Self-talk

Everybody talks to themselves, aloud or silently. Try not talking aloud to yourself on the course – your fellow players may brain you if you disturb their concentration at address – but talk to your inner self, and use this self-talk in a positive way, creating a vision of yourself scoring well and enjoying your game.

Self-talk that is encouraging and boosts the ego will result in better play. Negative self-talk and recriminations (all too often spoken aloud, to everyone else's annoyance) simply build up the negative side of that mental bank account.

Of course, ego-boosting self-talk must be realistic. Remember that you cannot fool your subconscious.

Good luck, bad luck, and superstition

Good luck and bad luck always balance out in the long run, so don't make a fuss if you seem to be having a run of bad luck. If your ball stops in a divot mark on the fairway, and you feel unfairly treated because of this stroke of misfortune (which, of course, only happens to you and never your fellow players), your chances of a good solid strike to get the ball out of the divot and well on its way to its target are minimal. "Bad luck" will only work if you let it get you down. If you accept it as a challenge, taking control of the situation by building up a good feeling about the shot you are going to take, then your concentration will be sharpened, your adrenalin will flow that little bit extra, and, summoning up that credit in your mental bank account, you can turn your "bad" luck into a positive experience.

How important is superstition? It can be a big help, if you can make it work positively for you. For instance, it can increase that feeling of *dejà vu* if you always play with a certain number ball. And that old cap of yours that always helps you on the back nine – you wouldn't be without it, would you? Be comfortable with your superstitions and they will help you; be uncomfortable with them, and they will make you choke.

After the round

Did you win? Well done! Don't be overmodest, but accept the congratulations of everyone. You set out to do this, and you have done it. Your mental bank account is in a very healthy state right now. This will stand you in good stead in future games.

But whether you win or lose, you *must* make an objective appraisal of your round, taking into account everything that happened, all the good and all the bad shots, savouring the good ones and working out what went wrong with the bad ones.

Make a list of the bad shots and check each one off against the following list, to find the reason.

Mental mistakes
1. Wrong choice of club?
2. Wrong shot to play?
3. Was my target projection poor?
4. Lack of decisiveness?
5. Did I set up a realistic goal for that shot?
6. Was it good course management to do that?
7. Self management could have been better there? Anger does not help!
8. Was I playing in the present tense?

Physical mistakes
1. Set-up and alignment routine was wrong.
2. Grip was wrong.
3. Incorrect tempo led to badly executed swing.

After the round is the best time to practise. You have your errors still clearly in your mind, and now you can practise those shots until you get them right.

Making a round analysis and then practising will help you to approach the next game with more knowledge, understanding, and confidence, and this will give you a better chance of succeeding.

The ultimate goal
It's not winning the Masters, or even the British Open. No. The ultimate goal of your game is to play to the best of your ability, given the course on the day and your present form, thus helping you to spend enjoyable hours on the golf course, in the company of good people, and in the fresh air.

Playing to the level of your ability means playing with knowledge, understanding, technical skill, and the right mental attitude. These are the four fundamentals of golf. Learn them, especially the last-mentioned, because this is the one about which most people do not think enough, and you are well on the way to being a proficient golfer who will continue to improve his or her game by practising and playing mental golf.

INDEX

A
angle of approach 18 – 19, 42

B
ball-flight laws 15 – 21, 41
beating that problem hole
    92 – 95

C
chipping 67 – 77
    simple chip 68 – 71
    uphill 72 – 73
concentration exercises 28 – 31
clubhead speed 19

D
déjà vu 28, 34
divot mark, playing from a
    110 – 111
downhill lie 102 – 103
draw 20, 112 – 113
drills 39

F
fade 20, 114 – 115
fairway bunker
    iron shot 132 – 133
    wood shot 134 – 135
fairway play 91 – 117
first-tee nerves 24, 25, 26, 27

G
golf fundamentals 15 – 21
golfing brain 11, 14
green, reading the 46 – 47
greenside bunker play
    122 – 128

H
hooking 25

I
iron clubs, long 108 – 109

L
long, running shot 116 – 117

M
mental attitudes 21, 22
mental barriers 24
mental training 10, 12, 23 – 31

N
notebook 34, 40

P
pitch
    high, soft 80 – 81
    short over a bunker 82 – 83
    wedge shot 86 – 87
    with a no. 8 or 9 iron
        84 – 85
    pitching 79 – 89
    position of clubface 17 – 18,
        21
planning a practice session 34
planning a round 155 – 156
practice "score card" 42 – 43
practising 32 – 43
pull 20
pull-hook 20
pull-slice 20
push 20
push-hook 20
push-slice 20
putting
    cross-handed grip 49
    off-green 58 – 65
    reverse overlap grip 48
routine 50

R
right choice of club 98 – 101
rough, playing in the 137 – 151
relaxing 22 – 23

S
sand, playing from 119 – 135
    lie, stance, swing 120
sand iron 119
    clubface 120
    swing 120
scrambling up the bank 76 – 77
self-knowledge 12 – 13
shot-length profile 12 – 13
sidehill lie 106, 107
sweet spot 19
swing path 15, 16, 21, 41, 42

T
target projection 23, 24, 26
thinking clearly 96 – 97

U
uphill lie 104 – 105

V
visualization 23, 24, 26

W
warming up 35 – 37
wood shot fairway) 92 – 93,
    112 – 113, 114, 115
wedge shot 86 – 87